8/81

Maria —
What better way
to celebrate your
wedding than with this
Cookbook and Bury!
Enjoy . . .
Jerry

Picnics for Lovers

GABRIELLE KIRSCHBAUM

Picnics for Lovers

Van Nostrand Reinhold Ltd., Toronto

New York, Cincinnati, London, Melbourne

©DESIGN BY *Frank Newfeld*

©ILLUSTRATIONS BY *Frank Newfeld and Dianne Richardson*

EDITING BY *Valerie Wyatt*

TYPESETTING BY *Fleet Typographers Limited*

PRINTED AND BOUND BY *The Hunter Rose Company*

Library of Congress Catalogue Number 79-57608

Canadian Cataloguing in Publication Data

Kirschbaum, Gabrielle, 1948 –
Picnics for lovers

ISBN 0-442-29726-2 bd.

1. Outdoor cookery.   2. Picnicking.   I. Title.

TX823.K57   641.5'78   C80-094155-1

80 81 82 83 84 85 86 10 9 8 7 6 5 4 3 2 1

PRINTED AND BOUND IN CANADA

Published in the United States of America by
Van Nostrand Reinhold Company, New York

*To my picnic
partner
for all times
and
for all places*

Table of Contents

Preface

Picnics are for lovers. Whether you're young or not-so-young, you may find yourself someday, someplace, surrendering to the powers of love. Instead of losing your appetite or sleep over it (one being definitely more regrettable than the other), why not celebrate your love with a picnic?

Set in a field of crocuses or by a crackling fire, on the stroke of midnight or in the softness of the dawn, a picnic for lovers becomes a love feast. Whatever the hour, the season or the setting, a lovers' picnic is always filled with a little magic. The secret ingredients are simple: a little time to prepare and enjoy your picnic and a little originality to tempt both your lover's palate and heart.

It was with love and fun and good food in mind that *Picnics for Lovers* was written, in the hope of enchanting you and your lover.

The picnics in this book are meant to appeal to both the beginner and the experienced cook, with an eye to an imaginative selection of common and more exotic foods. Most of the ingredients are readily available, but some will take you to specialty shops, delicatessens or gourmet stores. Be sure to take along your lover to share in the enjoyment of shopping for fresh coffee beans, homemade bread, meats and cheeses from around the world, fresh fish, fruits and vegetables. Make the preparation of your feast an adventure in itself!

Whether you have spontaneously decided to have a picnic, or have been mischievously planning one for a while, let your imagination take over. Don't wait for a sunny afternoon to go on your picnic – share an indoor breakfast on a rainy morning, unpack a knapsack and lunch in the shelter of a snow cabin, or bring out the china and crystal and have a midnight feast in front of the fireplace.

Spring, summer, fall and winter – *Picnics for Lovers* covers all seasons, and all possibilities.

Combining food and love is an ancient tradition, immortalized in poems, songs and plays. No modern-day celebration of food and love would be complete without some mention of "love foods." The last chapter of *Picnics for Lovers* describes some of the more legendary aphrodisiacs and the menus are sprinkled liberally with them.

Picnics for Lovers was a particularly enjoyable book to prepare – especially the testing! A great deal of enthusiasm, hard work, friendship and love on the part of friends and family went into this book, and I am very grateful to all involved. In particular, I would like to thank Margie Gill for her testing, proofreading and editorial advice, Halina Walter for her excellent technical help, Ilse Kyssa from The Pantry in Ottawa for her research materials on herbs and spices, Valerie Wyatt for her editing, and the team at Van Nostrand Reinhold, especially Laurie Coulter. Special mention goes to Linda Thom, Grande Diplômée du Cordon Bleu, Paris, and owner of L'Académie de Cuisine cooking school in Ottawa, who was the professional consultant for this book and whose expertise, advice and friendship I appreciate very much. To dispel any thoughts that *Picnics for Lovers* was prepared solely by women, I am happy to thank Richard Dukes and Don Thom for their help.

And to all the other picnic lovers I can't mention here, I send you a kiss.

G.K.
Ottawa, 1980

8

A Midsummer Night's Dream

A Picnic in the Moonlight

MENU

KIR ROYAL

AVOCADO SOUP

GAMBAS CON JEREZ
(SHRIMPS IN SHERRY)

DRY WHITE SPANISH WINE

TOMATOES WITH HERBS

SABAYON

A moonlit balcony, candles fluttering in the wind, and an Andalusian guitarist playing poignant love ballads. A perfect setting for this romantic picnic. Of course, if all the dark-eyed gypsies in town have left for the weekend, let a classical record be your serenade.

Kir Royal

| | | champagne |
| 2 tbsp | 30 mL | crème de cassis |

In two fluted champagne glasses, combine the crème de cassis with well-chilled champagne. Serve.

Avocado Soup

	1	ripe avocado
1 cup	250 mL	chicken stock
1/4 cup	60 mL	heavy or sour cream
		juice of 1/2 lemon
1 tbsp	15 mL	chopped fresh parsley
	1	mint leaf
		dash of cayenne pepper
		salt and pepper to taste
	2	mint leaves for garnish

Cut the avocado in halves and remove the stone. Scoop the flesh of the avocado into a blender and add the chicken stock, cream, lemon juice, half of the parsley, and the mint leaf. Cover and blend until smooth. Add the cayenne pepper and season to taste. Chill and garnish with the remaining parsley and mint leaves.

Gambas con Jerez

	1	medium-sized onion, finely chopped
	1	garlic clove, finely chopped
1 tsp	5 mL	olive oil
1/2 lb	250 g	fresh or thawed medium-sized shrimps
		pinch of saffron
		salt and pepper to taste
1/3 cup	75 mL	sherry
		rice

Gently sauté the onion and garlic in the olive oil until transparent. Add the shrimps, saffron, salt and pepper and cook over medium heat for about 5 minutes. Pour in the sherry and simmer for another 5 minutes. Serve on a bed of rice with a bottle of white wine.

Tomatoes with Herbs

4		ripe tomatoes, sliced
1 tbsp	15 mL	chopped fresh basil, thyme and dill, combined

Sprinkle garden-fresh tomatoes with basil for passion, thyme to ward off melancholy and dill for its magical properties.

Sabayon

3		egg yolks
1/4 cup	60 mL	sugar
1/4 cup	60 mL	marsala wine
		rind of 1 lemon, grated
		dash of powdered vanilla

Combine the egg yolks and sugar in a double boiler or stainless steel bowl. Over simmering water, whisk the mixture until it becomes fluffy. Add the marsala, grated lemon rind and vanilla. Continue to whisk vigorously until the sauce is very thick and creamy. (Be careful not to let the sauce come to a boil, or it will curdle.) Serve warm in small china cups.

Sing again, with your dear voice revealing
A tone
Of some world far from ours,
Where music and moonlight and feeling
Are one.
PERCY BYSSHE SHELLEY

Rendezvous at the Old Mill

MENU

CRAB SALAD
DRY WHITE WINE
SALAMI AND TOMATO ON RYE
DRY RED WINE
CAMEMBERT CHEESE
CHERRIES AND GRAPES

Egg salad sandwiches and carrot sticks are fine, but with a cool river or stream to keep your white wine chilled, and a little imagination, an ordinary picnic can be transformed into a love feast for two.

Crab Salad

6 oz	187 g	can of crab meat
2 tbsp	30 mL	Homemade Mayonnaise, see below
	4	green olives, chopped
1 tbsp	15 mL	finely chopped shallots
		juice of 1/2 lemon
		salt and freshly ground pepper
		lettuce leaves for garnish

Mix the crab, mayonnaise, olives, shallots and lemon juice in a bowl. Add salt and lots of freshly ground pepper. Serve on a bed of lettuce, accompanied with a half bottle of chilled dry white wine.

13

Homemade Mayonnaise

	1	egg
1/4 tsp	1.25 mL	Dijon mustard
1/2 tsp	2.5 mL	salt
		freshly ground pepper to taste
1 cup	250 mL	oil
		lemon juice

Combine the first 4 ingredients in a blender and mix for about 30 seconds. Continue to blend while adding the oil in a thin stream. As the mixture begins to thicken, pour in the oil a little faster. Thin as necessary with lemon juice. Cover the mayonnaise and store in the refrigerator. Homemade mayonnaise should keep for 3 to 4 days, chilled.

Salami and Tomato on Rye

2 tbsp	30 mL	Homemade Mayonnaise
	4	thick slices of dark rye bread
	6	slices of pepper salami
		bunch of fresh watercress
	1	tomato, sliced
		salt and pepper to taste

Spread the mayonnaise on the bread and make 2 sandwiches with 3 slices of salami each. Add some watercress and tomato slices and season with salt and pepper.

Complete your love feast with red wine, a wedge of warm, ripe Camembert and some cherries and grapes.

Breathless, we flung us on the windy hill,
Laughed in the sun, and kissed the lovely grass.
RUPERT BROOKE

14

A Touch of Class in a Secluded Spot

MENU

CANTALOUPE SOUP
COLD ROASTED TARRAGON CHICKEN
GARDEN VEGETABLES WITH HERB DIP
CHAMPAGNE
FRESH STRAWBERRIES

If you're tired of roughing it in the bush, pack a hamper with linen napkins, crystal goblets, silver and china, and treat your lover to a picnic with a touch of class.

Cantaloupe Soup

	1	ripe cantaloupe, peeled and cubed
1/4 cup	60 mL	chopped, peeled grapes
1 cup	250 mL	water
1/4 cup	60 mL	sherry or dry white wine
1 tsp	5 mL	sugar
	4	fresh mint leaves
		juice of 1 lemon
2 tbsp	30 mL	natural yoghurt
1 tsp	5 mL	pomegranate seeds for garnish

In a saucepan, combine the cantaloupe, grapes, water, sherry or wine, sugar and 2 mint leaves. Bring to a boil, then reduce the heat and simmer for 10 minutes. Cool and purée the soup in a blender. Mix in the lemon juice and chill. Pour into bowls, top with natural yoghurt and garnish with the remaining 2 mint leaves and the pomegranate seeds.

Cold Roasted Tarragon Chicken

3-1/2 lb	1.6 kg	chicken
		salt and freshly ground pepper
3 tbsp	45 mL	butter
2 tbsp	30 mL	finely chopped fresh tarragon (half quantity, if dried)

Preheat the oven to 375°F (190°C). Sprinkle the cavity of the chicken with salt and pepper. Dot the skin with half the butter. Cream the tarragon with the remaining butter and spoon into the chicken.

Place the chicken in a covered roasting pan and cook for 1 hour, basting often. Remove the lid and broil for 3 to 4 minutes for added color and crispness. Let cool, then refrigerate. Serve cold with champagne.

Garden Vegetables with Herb Dip

1/2 cup	125 mL	sour cream
1 tbsp	15 mL	finely chopped fresh parsley
1 tsp	5 mL	finely chopped fresh basil (half quantity, if dried)
1 tsp	5 mL	finely chopped fresh mint (half quantity, if dried)
		juice of 1/2 lemon
		salt and pepper
	6	cherry tomatoes
	1/2	small cauliflower, broken into florets
	2	carrots, cut into sticks
	2	shallots
	1	green pepper, seeded and cut into sticks

To make the dip, mix the first 6 ingredients together and refrigerate until ready to use. Serve with prepared vegetables.

Fresh Strawberries

1/2 lb	250 g	strawberries
		juice of 1/2 lemon
1 tbsp	15 mL	sugar

Wash, hull and slice the strawberries. Sprinkle the lemon juice and sugar over them just before serving.

A Taste of the Canadian Wild

MENU

CREAM OF ASPARAGUS SOUP
SALMON STEAKS WITH HERB MAYONNAISE
SPINACH SALAD
BAKE-APPLE OR RASPBERRY PIE

A secluded cabin in the woods, a crackling fire, a cold bottle of Inniskillin Chardonnay and some Bruce Cockburn playing in the background. Put these ingredients together and you have the makings for a romance, Canadian-style.

Cream of Asparagus Soup

1/2 lb	250 g	fresh asparagus
	1	onion, finely chopped
1 tbsp	15 mL	butter
1 tbsp	15 mL	flour
2 cups	500 mL	chicken stock
		salt, pepper and nutmeg to taste
		dash of cayenne pepper
1/4 cup	60 mL	heavy cream

Cook the asparagus in a large skillet of boiling salted

18

water until tender-crisp (approximately 7 to 12 minutes). Drain. Remove and reserve the tips. Chop the asparagus stalks.

Sauté the onion in the butter until transparent and mix in the chopped asparagus stalks. Add the flour and stir gently. Gradually pour in the chicken stock. Add the salt, pepper, nutmeg and cayenne pepper and simmer for 30 minutes.

Purée the soup in a blender, adding the cream. Serve hot, garnished with the asparagus tips.

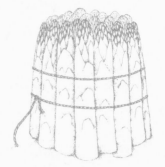

Salmon Steaks with Herb Mayonnaise

2 tbsp	30 mL	butter
1 tsp	5 mL	chopped fresh parsley
1/2 tsp	2.5 mL	chopped fresh marjoram (half quantity, if dried)
	1	onion, finely chopped
		juice of 1/2 lemon
		salt and pepper to taste
	2	fresh or thawed salmon steaks (1 in. or 2.5 cm thick)
		Herb Mayonnaise, see below

To prepare the salmon, cream together the butter, parsley, marjoram, onion, lemon juice, salt and pepper. Brush both sides of the salmon steaks generously with this mixture and grill over the fireplace or barbecue for 5 minutes on each side. Serve the salmon hot with the chilled herb mayonnaise.

Herb Mayonnaise

1/2 cup	125 mL	Homemade Mayonnaise, page 14
1 tsp	5 mL	finely chopped fresh chives (half quantity, if dried)
1/2 tsp	2.5 mL	finely chopped fresh tarragon (half quantity, if dried)
1 tbsp	15 mL	finely chopped fresh parsley
	1	garlic clove, finely chopped
1 tsp	5 mL	finely chopped fresh dill (half quantity, if dried)
		dash of paprika
		salt and pepper to taste

To make the herb mayonnaise, combine all the ingredients and chill.

19

Spinach Salad

fresh spinach leaves for 2
juice of 1/2 lime
salt and pepper to taste

Wash the spinach thoroughly under cold water and drain well. Sprinkle with lime juice, salt and pepper. Serve immediately.

Bake-Apple or Raspberry Pie

3 cups	750 mL	bake-apple berries or raspberries
2/3 cup	140 g	sugar
1 tbsp	15 mL	flour
		juice of 1/2 lemon
1/2 tsp	2.5 mL	nutmeg
1 tbsp	15 mL	heavy cream
		Pie Pastry for a double-crust pie, see below

Preheat the oven to 375°F (190°C). Combine the first 5 ingredients to make the filling and spoon into the bottom pie shell. Cover with the top crust and brush with the heavy cream. Bake for 40 minutes. Serve hot or cold.

Pie Pastry

2 cups	180 g	cake and pastry flour
1/2 tsp	2.5 mL	salt
2/3 cup	160 g	shortening, cut into bits
1/4 cup	60 mL	cold water

On a floured board or counter, mix the flour, salt and shortening together with the tips of your fingers. (Make sure your fingers are cold; if necessary, run them under cold water.) The flour mixture should resemble rolled oats. Add the water, a little at a time, and mix lightly. Form the pastry into a ball, cover with waxed paper and refrigerate for at least 1 hour. Makes sufficient pastry for 1 double-crust pie.

For Summertime Lovers

MENU

GAZPACHO
GRILLED PORK CHOPS
SWEET APPLE AND ONION RINGS

Some summer evenings seem to have been created especially for lovers. Summer magic can happen anywhere, even in a city backyard. Just light the barbecue, cut a rose and sit back and enjoy these summer delights.

Gazpacho

3/4 cup	175 mL	peeled and chopped cucumber
	1	onion, finely chopped
	1	garlic clove, finely chopped
	1	green pepper, seeded and chopped
	1	large tomato, peeled, seeded and chopped
	1/2	celery stalk, chopped
1/2 tsp	2.5 mL	chopped fresh oregano (half quantity, if dried)
1/2 tsp	2.5 mL	chopped fresh basil (half quantity, if dried)
1/2 tsp	2.5 mL	chopped fresh chives
1 tbsp	15 mL	vinegar
1 tbsp	15 mL	olive oil
2 cups	500 mL	tomato juice
		salt and pepper to taste
1/2 cup	125 mL	cubed tomatoes, celery, green pepper and cucumber, combined

Combine all the ingredients, except the cubed vegetables, in a blender and blend until smooth. Chill thoroughly. Serve cold, topped with the cubed vegetables.

Grilled Pork Chops

1 tbsp	15 mL	vegetable oil
		juice of 1/2 lemon
1/2 tsp	2.5 mL	chopped fresh thyme (half quantity, if dried)
		salt and pepper to taste
	2	lean butterfly pork chops

Combine the first four ingredients and brush over the pork chops. Grill for 15 to 20 minutes on each side, or until the pork chops are cooked throughout. Accompany with sweet apple and onion rings.

Sweet Apple and Onion Rings

2		tart apples, peeled, cored and cut into rings
2		onions, peeled and cut into rings
2 tbsp	30 mL	butter, softened
2 tbsp	30 mL	brown sugar

Place the apple and onion rings on a sheet of foil. Cream together the butter and brown sugar and spread over the apple and onion rings. Wrap in foil and cook over grey coals for 8 to 10 minutes, or until tender.

Oh! The Summer Night
Has a smile of light,
And she sits on a sapphire throne.
BRYAN WALLER PROCTER

23

Hitch-hikers' Picnic
for Eloping Lovers

MENU

CLAMATO JUICE
SARDINES, TOMATOES AND CUCUMBER ON
PITA BREAD
CREAM CHEESE AND PECANS ON RAISIN BREAD
CARROT AND CELERY STICKS
SUMMER FRUIT AND DARK CHOCOLATE

If you're in a hurry to escape with your loved one and find that you haven't packed the champagne and escargots (or you can't afford them), don't panic. You can still tempt each other with a tasty and original picnic for loving and leaving together. Start with spicy clamato juice and finish with crisp vegetables and ripe summer fruit.

Sardines, Tomatoes and Cucumber on Pita Bread

1 tbsp	15 mL	Homemade Mayonnaise, page 14
	1	pita (flat Middle Eastern bread), cut in halves
	1	small can sardines
	1	large tomato, sliced
	1/2	cucumber, sliced
		salt and pepper to taste

Spread the mayonnaise in the pocket of the pita bread and stuff with the sardines, tomatoes and cucumber. Season to taste.

Cream Cheese and Pecans on Raisin Bread

	4	slices raisin bread
1/4 cup	60 mL	cream cheese
2 tbsp	30 mL	chopped pecans

Spread the cream cheese on the raisin bread and sprinkle with the chopped pecans.

Come live with me, and be my love;
And we will all the pleasures prove
That valleys, groves, hills, and fields,
Woods or steepy mountain yields.
CHRISTOPHER MARLOWE

25

Never on Sunday

MENU

OUZO

MOUSSAKA

TZATZIKI
(CUCUMBER AND YOGHURT SALAD)

BAKLAVA

Picture yourself in a taverna on Crete with joyful bouzouki music playing in the background. Start with an ouzo, then throw yourself into the enjoyment of Greek food at its sensuous best. Be sure to save room for a piece of baklava, a gift from the gods.

Moussaka

	1	medium-sized eggplant (aubergine), thinly sliced (1/2 in. or 1 cm thick)
4 tbsp	60 mL	olive oil
	1	onion, finely chopped
3/4 lb	375 g	lean ground lamb
1/4 tsp	1.25 mL	cinnamon
		salt and freshly ground pepper to taste
	1	tomato, peeled, seeded and finely chopped
2 tbsp	30 mL	tomato paste
	1	garlic clove, finely chopped
1/4 tsp	1.25 mL	dried oregano
1 tbsp	15 mL	finely chopped Italian parsley (flat-leaf)
3 tbsp	45 mL	freshly grated Parmesan cheese
		Béchamel Sauce, see below

Sprinkle the eggplant with salt and set aside for 30 minutes. Drain and pat dry. Fry in half of the oil, then set aside to drain on paper towels.

Fry the onion in the remaining oil until golden. Stir in the ground lamb and the cinnamon, salt and pepper and fry until well browned. Drain off the fat. Add the tomato, tomato paste, garlic, oregano and parsley. Cook over medium heat for 15 minutes, or until all the liquid is absorbed. Preheat the oven to 375°F (190°C).

Line a deep greased baking dish with half of the eggplant slices and sprinkle with a third of the cheese. Pour in the lamb mixture and cover with the remaining eggplant slices. Sprinkle again with a third of the cheese. Pour béchamel sauce over the eggplant and top with the remaining cheese. Bake in the oven for 40 minutes, then turn the oven to broil. Broil for 3 minutes, until the top becomes golden.

Béchamel Sauce

1 tbsp	15 mL	butter
1 tbsp	15 mL	flour
1/2 cup	125 mL	hot milk
	1	egg yolk, beaten

Melt the butter in a saucepan, add the flour and cook over low heat for 3 to 5 minutes. Slowly pour in the hot milk, stirring constantly until it boils. Simmer until the sauce becomes thick. Remove from the heat and stir in the beaten egg yolk.

Tzatziki

	1	medium-sized cucumber, peeled and very finely sliced
2 tbsp	30 mL	yoghurt
	1	garlic clove, crushed
1 tsp	5 mL	olive oil
1 tsp	5 mL	vinegar

Salt the sliced cucumber and set aside for 30 minutes. Drain and combine with the remaining ingredients. Serve chilled with the moussaka.

Baklava

1/4 cup	60 mL	coarsely chopped walnuts
1/4 cup	60 mL	coarsely chopped pistachios
1 tsp	5 mL	sugar
1/4 cup	60 mL	sweet butter, melted
	6	phyllo pastry sheets
1-1/2 cups	375 mL	water
1 cup	250 mL	sugar
2 tbsp	30 mL	honey
	1	cinnamon stick
		juice of 1/2 lemon

Preheat the oven to 350°F (180°C). Combine the nuts and the 1 tsp (5 mL) sugar in a bowl and set aside.

Using a pastry brush, butter a small loaf pan. Tear a phyllo sheet into 3 pieces. (Keep the remaining dough in a damp tea towel to prevent it from drying out as you work.) Place one piece on the bottom of the mold and brush it with butter. Repeat with more pieces of phyllo pastry, tearing another sheet into 3 pieces, until you have 6 layers. Be sure to butter each layer.

Sprinkle half of the nut mixture on top. Repeat with 6 more layers of buttered phyllo and the remaining nut mixture. Repeat with 6 more layers of buttered pastry. Butter the top of the last layer. Score the pastry into 2 in. (5 cm) squares and bake for 40 minutes, or until golden.

To make the syrup, combine the water, 1 cup (250 mL) sugar, honey, cinnamon and lemon juice in a saucepan. Heat to boiling, then reduce the heat and simmer for 20 minutes. Remove the cinnamon stick.

When the baklava is baked, pour all the syrup over it. Let cool, then refrigerate. As baklava is very sweet, serve your lover a small piece at a time.

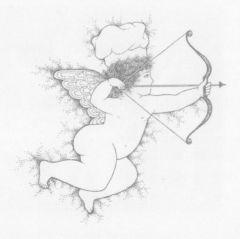

Breakfast at Tiffany's

MENU

CHAMPLEMOUSSE
PAPAYA WITH YOGHURT
BLUEBERRY MUFFINS
JASMINE TEA

It doesn't only happen in the movies – not if you do it right. Try champagne for breakfast; cold, frothy champagne mixed with fresh grapefruit juice. Follow with a fresh papaya, a succulent tropical fruit, filled with yoghurt, and accompany with the gentle aroma of jasmine tea. George Peppard never had it so good!

Champlemousse

1		grapefruit, freshly squeezed
1 tsp	5 mL	sugar
		champagne, well chilled
2		twists of lime

In two fluted champagne glasses, mix fresh grapefruit juice and sugar. Fill the glasses with champagne and add the twists of lime. Serve immediately.

Papaya with Yoghurt

1		ripe papaya
4 tbsp	60 mL	natural yoghurt

Slice a papaya in halves and remove the seeds. Fill each half with yoghurt and serve immediately.

Blueberry Muffins

4 tbsp	60 mL	butter
1/3 cup	75 mL	sugar
1		egg, beaten
1 cup	250 mL	milk
2 cups	500 mL	unsifted cake and pastry flour
1/2 tsp	2.5 mL	salt
1 tbsp	15 mL	baking powder
3/4 cup	175 mL	fresh or thawed blueberries

Preheat the oven to 400°F (205°C). Cream the butter and sugar together until smooth. Stir in the beaten egg and milk. In another bowl, sift together the flour, salt and baking powder. Make a well in the center of the dry ingredients and pour the first mixture into it. Stir only until the flour mixture is dampened. The batter should be lumpy. Fold in the berries. Fill 12 lined or well-greased muffin cups two-thirds full. Bake 20 to 25 minutes. Serve warm with sweet butter and a pot of delicate jasmine tea.

A Picnic by the Seaside

MENU

MOULES MARINIÈRE
FRENCH BREAD
BATAVIA SALAD
GOAT'S CHEESE
APRICOT TARTE

The Normandy seaside towns of Deauville, Honfleur and Cabourg have long been the setting for clandestine love affairs and romantic rendezvous. If you and your lover can't make it to France for a superb French feast, why not bring a little Normandy to your seacoast?

Moules Marinière

2-1/4 lb	1 kg	mussels
2 tbsp	30 mL	butter
	1	onion, finely chopped
1 tbsp	15 mL	chopped shallots, including stems
1/2 cup	125 mL	white wine
		juice of 1/2 lemon
1 tbsp	15 mL	chopped fresh parsley
1/2 tsp	2.5 mL	dried thyme
	1	bay leaf
		salt and pepper to taste

Scrub the mussels thoroughly under cold running water, removing any seaweed, sand or beard. Discard any open or broken mussels.

Combine all of the ingredients, except the mussels, in a pot. Cover and bring to a boil. Add the mussels and cook for about 3 or 4 minutes, or until the shells have opened. Remove the mussels from the pot and keep warm. Strain the stock through a sieve lined with a dampened tea towel or folded cheesecloth to get rid of any sand. Pour the stock over the mussels and serve hot with French bread.

Batavia Salad

Try a lovely fresh Batavia salad, Boston lettuce tossed lightly with a spicy vinaigrette dressing (see below), and follow it with goat's cheese, one of nature's aphrodisiacs.

Vinaigrette Dressing

1/2 tbsp	7.5 mL	wine vinegar
1-1/2 tbsp	22.5 mL	olive oil
1/4 tsp	1.25 mL	Dijon mustard
	1/2	small garlic clove, crushed
		juice of 1/4 lemon
		salt and freshly ground pepper

Combine the ingredients for the vinaigrette dressing, shake well and chill. Pour over the salad just before serving.

Apricot Tarte

2 oz 1/2 stick	sweet butter, cut into 1/2 in. (1 cm) pieces
1 cup 250 mL	cake and pastry flour
1/4 tsp 1.25 mL	salt
2 tbsp 30 mL	water
3/4 lb 375 mL	apricots, sliced into eighths
2 tbsp 30 mL	apricot jelly
1 tbsp 15 mL	freshly squeezed lemon juice
1 tbsp 15 mL	calvados (apple brandy from Normandy)

On a floured counter or board, mix the butter, flour and salt together with the tips of your fingers. (Make sure your fingers are cold; if necessary run them under cold water.) The butter and flour mixture should resemble rolled oats. Make a well in the center of the flour mixture and little by little add the water, stirring it into the flour with a circular motion of a finger. Pat the dough into a mound, and then, with the heel of your hand, smear all the dough away from you in a single motion. Fold the dough away from you and flatten with a rolling pin. Repeat, folding the dough to the left and to the right.

Pat the dough into a ball and sprinkle with flour. Cover with waxed paper and refrigerate for at least 2 hours.

Preheat the oven to 425°F (220°C). When the pastry is cold, roll it out on a floured counter and mold it into a pie pan. Fill with apricots and bake for 35 minutes.

When the pie is almost baked, combine the apricot jelly, lemon juice and half of the calvados in a saucepan and cook, stirring, over medium heat until the mixture reaches a sauce-like consistency. Remove the pie from the oven and pour the apricot sauce over it. Bake the pie for 5 minutes longer. Sprinkle with the remaining calvados before serving.

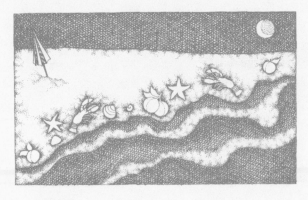

A Picnic for Love

MENU

OYSTER SOUP
ZUCCHINI STUFFED WITH LAMB AND PINE NUTS
LIGHT RED WINE
FRESH FIGS IN CREAM
CHAMPAGNE

If you can believe what you read, the aphrodisiacal qualities of the foods on this menu should assure you a very long and active love life. Oysters, pine nuts and figs are rumored to rate high on the scale of love foods. However, even skeptics will enjoy this unusual combination of tastes and textures.

Oyster Soup

4 tbsp	60 mL	butter
	1	onion, finely chopped
	18	fresh oysters, with their liquid
1 tbsp	15 mL	chopped fresh parsley
		salt and pepper to taste
		pinch of cayenne pepper
		thyme to taste
2 tbsp	30 mL	flour
1/2 cup	125 mL	white wine
1/2 cup	125 mL	milk or fish stock
1 cup	250 mL	table cream
	1	egg yolk, beaten

Melt half the butter in a saucepan. Add the onion, oysters, oyster liquid, herbs and spices. Simmer for 3 to 4 minutes, or until the edges of the oysters curl. Set aside.

In another saucepan, melt the remaining butter. Stir in the flour to make a white roux. Gradually add the wine, milk or fish stock, and cream, stirring constantly. Mix in the beaten egg yolk. Do not let the mixture boil or it will curdle. Add the oysters and broth and stir constantly for 5 minutes. Serve hot.

Zucchini Stuffed with Lamb and Pine Nuts

	1	medium-sized zucchini
	1	onion, finely chopped
1 tbsp	15 mL	butter
1/4 lb	125 g	ground lamb
1 tbsp	15 mL	pine nuts
1 tbsp	15 mL	chopped fresh basil (half quantity, if dried)
1 tsp	5 mL	chopped fresh rosemary (half quantity, if dried)
1 tsp	5 mL	chopped fresh marjoram (half quantity, if dried)
1/2 tsp	2.5 mL	crushed coriander seeds
		salt and pepper to taste
	1	small tomato, cubed
		juice of 1/2 lemon

1 cup	250 mL	tomato juice
2 tbsp	30 mL	freshly grated Parmesan and Mozzarella cheese, combined

Slice the zucchini in halves and hollow out the center of each half. Steam the zucchini halves for 5 minutes, or until they are just beginning to soften.

Meanwhile, sauté the onion in the butter over medium heat. Add the lamb, pine nuts and spices and cook for about 15 minutes, or until the meat is browned, stirring occasionally. Add the cubed tomato and cook for another 2 to 3 minutes. Sprinkle with the lemon juice.

Preheat the oven to 400°F (205°C). Fill the zucchini halves with the lamb mixture. Place in a skillet and pour in the tomato juice. Bring to a boil and simmer for 15 minutes, or until the zucchini is tender. Baste the meat with tomato juice as it cooks. Sprinkle with the grated cheese, transfer to the oven and bake until the cheese has melted. Serve hot with a light red wine.

Fresh Figs in Cream

4		fresh figs, peeled and sliced
1 tbsp	15 mL	kirsch
		juice of 1/4 lemon
1/2 cup	125 mL	whipping cream
		pinch of grated nutmeg

Sprinkle the figs with the kirsch and lemon juice. Whip the cream until stiff and blend in the grated nutmeg. Fold the figs into the cream and chill for several hours before serving. Delicious with chilled champagne!

Summer set lip to earth's bosom bare,
And left the flushed print in a poppy there.
FRANCIS THOMPSON

In the Morning Mist

MENU

FRESH BERRIES

GRILLED TROUT

FRENCH TOAST WITH MAPLE SYRUP

COFFEE

Silent waters, the whirr of a casting line, the crackling of a wood fire. Quiet moments in the morning mist. Take a walk in the woods to pick fresh berries, then light a fire to grill or pan fry the morning's catch of trout.

Fresh Berries

Pick a bowlful of raspberries, blueberries or wild strawberries. Wash, hull, sprinkle with lemon juice and serve with cream.

Grilled Trout

	2	trout, washed and cleaned
2 tbsp	30 mL	butter
1 tbsp	15 mL	oil
		juice of 1/2 lemon
		salt and pepper to taste

To pan fry the trout, melt the butter in a skillet, and when bubbling, add the fish and cook for 5 to 8 minutes on each side, or until done. Sprinkle with the lemon juice and season with salt and pepper. Serve hot.

To grill the fish, rub the oil over the grill and the butter over the trout. Grill for 5 to 8 minutes on each side, or until cooked. Season with salt and pepper. Serve hot, sprinkled with the lemon juice.

French Toast with Maple Syrup

	2	eggs
1 tsp	5 mL	milk
		salt and pepper to taste
2 tbsp	30 mL	butter
	4	slices of crusty French or Italian bread
		maple syrup

Beat the eggs and milk together and season with salt and pepper. Melt the butter in a skillet. Dip the bread into the egg mixture and fry in the bubbling butter for 5 minutes on each side, or until crispy and golden. Serve hot, topped with maple syrup, and then enjoy a steaming mug of coffee.

The Sandman and You

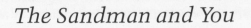

MENU

LOBSTERS WITH DRAWN BUTTER
DRY WHITE WINE
FRESH PEACHES

Build a fire on the beach and invite the sandman to share a feast of fresh lobster. Crack the lobster open on a rock, dip the flesh into melted butter and watch the tide erase the sandman's footsteps. No one but you need know he was there.

Lobsters with Drawn Butter

2 live lobsters
   water
1 stick of butter

   Place a large pot filled with water over a hot fire and bring to a boil. (Use salt water, if you can.) Place the live lobsters, head first, into the boiling water and cook for 8 to 10 minutes. Remove from the water. The lobsters will be a lovely orange-red color.

   Meanwhile, melt the butter in a small saucepan. Crack the lobster shells, pull out the meat and dip it into the hot butter. Heavenly! Enjoy your feast with a glass of dry white wine and follow it with fresh peaches.

Corn Roast at Your Hideaway

MENU

CORN ON THE COB
HAMBURGERS WITH MUSHROOM SAUCE OR
SPICY HAMBURGERS
HOT DOGS AND ROQUEFORT CHEESE
WATERMELON

If, deep down inside, you and your lover aren't partial to escargots and truffles and raw oysters, escape to the privacy of your hideaway and enjoy a traditional North American picnic.

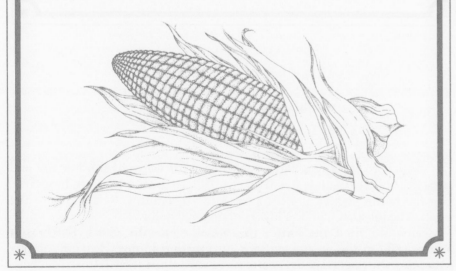

Corn on the Cob

2 cobs of corn
1/2 cup 125 mL water

Keep the corn in its jacket. Sprinkle water over the husk and cook over low coals for about 20 minutes or until the husk is well browned and the corn is steamed tender.

Hamburgers with Mushroom Sauce

1/2 lb	250 g	ground beef
1 tbsp	15 mL	sour cream
2 tbsp	30 mL	chopped chives
		dash of curry powder
2 tbsp	30 mL	crushed garlic croutons
		salt and freshly ground pepper
		Mushroom Sauce, see below

Combine the ingredients and divide into 2 patties. Cook slowly on both sides on the barbecue until done. Top with mushroom sauce.

Mushroom Sauce

1		onion, in thin rings
1/2 cup	125 mL	chopped mushrooms
1 tsp	5 mL	butter
1/4 cup	60 mL	red wine
		salt and freshly ground pepper to taste

Gently sauté the onion and mushrooms in butter until tender. Add the wine and simmer for 5 minutes longer. Season to taste. Pour over the hot hamburgers and serve with crusty bread.

Spicy Hamburgers

1/2 lb	250 g	ground beef
2 tbsp	30 mL	chopped shallots
	1	garlic clove, finely chopped
1 tbsp	15 mL	finely chopped fresh parsley
1/4 tsp	1.25 mL	crushed dried chilies
	1	egg
		dash of tabasco sauce
		salt and pepper to taste
1 cup	250 mL	chopped tomato, zucchini and Spanish onion, combined for garnish
		sesame buns

Combine the first 8 ingredients and divide into 2 patties. Cook slowly on the barbecue for about 6 minutes on each side, or until done to your taste. Top the hamburgers with the chopped tomato, zucchini and Spanish onion and serve in a sesame bun brushed with mustard, ketchup or relish.

Hot Dogs and Roquefort Cheese

	4	wieners
	2	pita (flat Middle Eastern bread)
		Dijon mustard
1/4 cup	60 mL	freshly grated Roquefort cheese

Grill the wieners on the barbecue. Cut the pita bread in halves and spread the insides sparingly with Dijon mustard. Fill with the wieners and top with cheese. Wrap in foil and place over the barbecue for five minutes to melt the cheese. Finish your meal with thick slices of juicy watermelon.

The evening star,
Love's harbinger.
JOHN MILTON

43

A Hammock for Two

MENU

GRILLED CHICKEN BREASTS
GARDEN SALAD
SUMMER DELIGHT
CHAMPAGNE

Who wants to spend time in the kitchen on a lazy summer night filled with sounds of crickets when you could be gently swaying in a hammock for two? Have your lover join you, make a wish upon a star and then prepare this simple yet delicious feast.

Grilled Chicken Breasts

1		whole chicken breast, split into two
		juice of 1 lemon
2 tbsp	30 mL	butter, softened
1/2 tsp	2.5 mL	dried rosemary
		salt and pepper to taste

Wash and pat dry the chicken breasts. Cream the lemon, butter, rosemary, salt and pepper and brush generously over the chicken. Grill the chicken for 30 to 40 minutes, turning frequently to avoid charring. Serve hot or cold.

Garden Salad

1/2		head lettuce, broken into bite-sized pieces
1		large tomato, sliced
1		medium-sized cucumber, sliced
1		medium-sized carrot, sliced
		peas from 6 pods
1		small zucchini, sliced
1 tbsp	15 mL	finely chopped fresh parsley
1 tbsp	15 mL	finely chopped fresh chives
		Vinaigrette Dressing, page 33

Combine the salad ingredients and toss with the vinaigrette dressing just before serving.

Summer Delight

1		ripe cantaloupe
1/4 cup	60 mL	fresh raspberries
1/4 cup	60 mL	fresh blueberries
1/4 cup	60 mL	champagne
		juice of 1/2 lime
2		mint leaves

Cut the cantaloupe in halves and remove the seeds and filaments. Combine the raspberries, blueberries, champagne and lime juice and fill the cantaloupe halves. Top with mint leaves. Serve well chilled with a glass of champagne.

Déjeuner sur l'Herbe

MENU

ARTICHOKE HEARTS
HOMEMADE PÂTÉ
BRIE AND PORT-SALUT CHEESE WITH BAGUETTES
DRY RED WINE
FRESH FIGS AND PEARS

Édouard Manet's famous painting "Déjeuner sur l'herbe" immortalizes the beauty of a summer's picnic. Find a secluded spot in a quiet park and enjoy this little French picnic.

merci, M. Manet

46

Artichoke Hearts

4 small artichokes
1 lemon
1 bay leaf
1/2 tsp 2.5 mL sea salt
Vinaigrette Dressing, page 33

Wash the artichokes. Cut the stems horizontally near the bases so that the artichokes will stand up. (Rub all cuts with lemon immediately to prevent discoloration.) Remove the tough outer layer of leaves. With a knife, cut off the tops of the artichokes and snip off the ends of the sharp leaves.

Set the artichokes upright in a pot with enough water to just cover them. Squeeze the juice from the lemon over the artichokes and drop the squeezed lemon into the water. Add the bay leaf and sea salt. Bring to a boil. Cook over medium heat for 20 to 30 minutes, or until a lower leaf can be pulled off easily and the meat on the base of the leaf is tender.

When the outer leaves indicate doneness, remove the artichokes from the water. Cool and then chill in the refrigerator. When the artichokes are well chilled, break off all the outer and inner leaves. Remove the feathery choke with a spoon or a knife and gently scrape clean the artichoke hearts. Serve the hearts cold topped with vinaigrette dressing.

Homemade Pâté

1/4 lb	125 g	bacon strips
2 tbsp	30 mL	shallots
1 tbsp	15 mL	butter
	4	bacon strips, chopped
1 tbsp	15 mL	chopped fresh parsley
		salt and pepper to taste
1 tbsp	15 mL	dried thyme, marjoram and tarragon, combined
1/2 lb	250 g	calf or baby beef liver, thinly sliced
2 tbsp	30 mL	cognac
	1	egg
	2	bay leaves
	3	bacon strips

Line a 3 cup (750 mL) pâté mold with the 1/4 lb (125 g) of bacon strips and chill. In a large frying pan, sauté the shallots in butter until transparent. Add the chopped bacon and parsley and season with the salt, pepper, thyme, marjoram and tarragon. Cook for 5 minutes over low heat. Add the liver and cognac and cook gently until browned.

Preheat the oven to 325°F (170°C). Transfer the cooked liver to a blender, add the egg and blend until smooth. Pour the mixture into the pâté mold. Place the bay leaves on top and seal the pâté with 3 bacon strips. Cover the mold with aluminum foil. Place in a pan of hot water (*bain marie*) and bake for 1 hour.

When cooked, place a 3 to 4 pound weight on the pâté. Cool and refrigerate overnight. The pâté is best if allowed to age for at least one week, but it may be eaten sooner.

To complete your meal, enjoy some Brie and Port-Salut with baguettes and a good bottle of dry red wine. Then close your eyes and taste the fresh figs and pears.

Once if I remember well,
my life was a feast where
all hearts opened and all
wines flowed.
ARTHUR RIMBAUD

AUTUMN
LEAVES

On a Bicycle Built for Two

MENU

TOMATO AND BASIL SOUP
CURRIED CHICKEN SUBMARINE SANDWICH
BANANAS AND COCONUT PIECES

When the fall colors reflect on the river and the nip in the air calls for a wool sweater, share a bicycle ride with your lover and pack a little summertime before bidding it a final adieu.

Tomato and Basil Soup

	1	large onion, finely chopped
	1	large garlic clove, finely chopped
1 tsp	5 mL	butter
2 tsp	10 mL	olive oil
	4	medium-sized tomatoes, peeled, seeded and cut up
2 tbsp	30 mL	finely chopped fresh basil (half quantity, if dried)
	1	bay leaf
2 tsp	10 mL	fresh mint (half quantity, if dried)
1 tbsp	15 mL	finely chopped fresh parsley
1 tsp	5 mL	salt
		freshly ground pepper
1/2 tsp	2.5 mL	sugar
		juice of 1/2 lemon
2 cups	500 mL	chicken stock
2 tbsp	30 mL	natural yoghurt

Over medium heat, fry the onion and garlic in butter and oil until transparent. Add the tomatoes, basil, bay leaf, mint, parsley, salt, lots of pepper, sugar and lemon juice. Cook for 3 to 5 minutes, or until the tomatoes begin to get soft. Pour in the stock, bring to a boil, then simmer for 15 minutes. Transfer to a blender and blend until smooth. Refrigerate. Mix in the yoghurt. Keep cold in a thermos.

Curried Chicken Submarine Sandwich

1 cup	250 mL	cooked chicken, cubed
2 tbsp	30 mL	Homemade Mayonnaise, page 14
	1	small apple, peeled and cubed
1 tbsp	15 mL	finely chopped fresh chives
		juice of 1/2 lemon
1 tsp	5 mL	curry powder
		pinch of cayenne pepper
		salt and pepper to taste

Combine all the ingredients and spread over horizontally sliced submarine buns or Italian or French baguettes.

Bananas and Coconut Pieces

Complete your picnic with ripe bananas and fresh coconut pieces. To crack a coconut, hammer a nail into the top of the coconut to make two holes. (You will notice there are three tender spots.) Drain the coconut of its milk and save for another recipe. Crack the coconut with a hammer.

For Those Who Are Game

MENU

PARTRIDGES WITH WILD RICE STUFFING
CIDER
SPINACH, MANDARIN AND AVOCADO SALAD

They say that in love and hunt, all is fair game. Escape
to a country retreat, pluck yourself a partridge and Lady
Luck is sure to smile on you.

Partridges with Wild Rice Stuffing

		1/2 onion, chopped
1/4 cup	60 mL	chopped fresh mushrooms
1 tbsp	15 mL	butter
1/4 cup	60 mL	slightly undercooked wild rice
		salt and pepper to taste
		1 brace of partridges, fresh or thawed
		juice of 1/2 lemon
		2 bacon slices
		1/2 onion, cut into thin rings
2 tbsp	30 mL	red Cinzano

Preheat the oven to 375°F (190°C). Over medium heat, sauté the chopped onion and mushrooms in the butter until they become tender. Add the rice and season with salt and pepper. Remove from the heat and set aside.

Wash and pat dry the two partridges. Sprinkle with salt and pepper. Stuff with the wild rice mixture. Secure with strings or skewers. Sprinkle the birds with lemon juice.

Cut each strip of bacon into 4 pieces. Cover the breast of each partridge with the 4 pieces of bacon. Place the onion rings in the bottom of a roasting pan. Put the partridges on the onion rings, pour in the Cinzano and cover.

Cook for 1 hour, basting often. Uncover and broil for 3 to 5 minutes until the bacon is crisp and the partridges are browned. Serve hot with chilled cider.

Spinach, Mandarin and Avocado Salad

		fresh spinach leaves for 2
		1 mandarin orange, peeled and sectioned
		1 small ripe avocado, peeled and cut into chunks
1 tbsp	15 mL	sunflower seeds, shelled
1 tbsp	15 mL	olive oil
		juice of 1/2 lemon
		salt and pepper to taste

Rinse the spinach leaves well, dry and tear into handsome pieces. Lightly combine the spinach, orange, avocado and sunflower seeds. Just before serving, sprinkle with the oil, lemon juice, salt and pepper, and toss.

In the Early Morning Rain

MENU

CANTALOUPE WITH BLUEBERRIES
SMOKED SALMON, CREAM CHEESE AND CAPERS ON
BROWN BREAD
COFFEE

The still grey of an early autumn morning with gentle rain falling against the window pane provides a touch of poetry for this feast of colors and flavors.

Cantaloupe with Blueberries

1		ripe cantaloupe
1 cup	250 mL	fresh blueberries
		juice of 1/2 lemon
		sugar
2		thin lemon slices

Cut the cantaloupe in halves and remove the seeds and filaments. Fill each half with blueberries and sprinkle with lemon and sugar. Serve cold, garnished with lemon slices.

Smoked Salmon, Cream Cheese and Capers on Brown Bread

2 tbsp	30 mL	cream cheese
2		slices of brown bread, cut in halves
2		slices of smoked salmon, cut in halves
1/2 tsp	2.5 mL	capers
		pepper

Spread the cream cheese on the bread. Top with the smoked salmon and capers and season with pepper. Serve with freshly brewed coffee.

Love consists in this, that two solitudes protect and touch and greet each other.
RAINER MARIA RILKE

A Picnic in the Leaves

MENU

ZUCCHINI AND TOMATO SOUP
TURKEY, CRANBERRIES AND CHOPPED PECANS ON
BROWN BREAD
BUTTER TARTS

A walk through the crackling leaves, an early sunset
gently bidding summer farewell – autumn brings its
own nostalgia and romance to lovers everywhere. For
this sentimental journey, pack a picnic filled with fall's
colors and goodness.

Zucchini and Tomato Soup

		1 onion, finely chopped
		1 large garlic clove, finely chopped
		1 - 2 zucchini, cut into 1/2 in. (1 cm) pieces
1 tbsp	15 mL	butter
1 tbsp	15 mL	chopped fresh basil (half quantity, if dried)
1 tsp	5 mL	chopped fresh thyme (half quantity, if dried)
		1 bay leaf
		salt and freshly ground pepper
		2 tomatoes, peeled, seeded and cut into wedges
2 cups	500 mL	chicken stock

Over medium heat, sauté the onion, garlic and zucchini in the butter until they begin to become tender. Add the basil, thyme, bay leaf, salt, lots of pepper and tomatoes. Cook for 3 to 5 minutes. Pour in the chicken stock, bring to a boil, then simmer for 5 minutes. Pour into a thermos so it will be hot when you're ready to enjoy it.

Turkey, Cranberries and Chopped Pecans on Brown Bread

		Homemade Mayonnaise, page 14
		cranberry sauce
		4 slices brown bread
		4 slices turkey
		salt and pepper to taste
2 tbsp	30 mL	chopped pecans

Spread mayonnaise and cranberry sauce on brown bread. Top with slices of turkey, season with salt and pepper and sprinkle with chopped pecans. Delicious!

Butter Tarts

3 tbsp	45 mL	soft butter
1/4 cup	60 mL	brown sugar
1/4 cup	60 mL	maple syrup
1 tbsp	15 mL	sour cream
	1	beaten egg
1/4 tsp	1.25 mL	vanilla
		juice of 1/4 lemon
		dash of nutmeg, cinnamon and salt
		Pie Pastry for 6 tart shells (see recipe for Pie Pastry, page 20, and use 1/2 quantity)

Preheat the oven to 425°F (220°C). Cream together the butter, sugar, maple syrup and sour cream. Add the egg, vanilla, lemon juice, nutmeg, cinnamon and salt. Fill the tart shells two-thirds full. Bake for 5 to 8 minutes, then reduce heat to 350°F (180°C) and bake for another 10 to 15 minutes, or until the pastry is pale golden.

For Market Lovers

MENU

RATATOUILLE
OMELETTE AUX FINES HERBES
CHEDDAR CHEESE AND APPLES

An open-air market abounding with garlic, tomatoes, zucchini, eggplant, pumpkin, apples and squash is a feast for the eyes – and for the palate. Why not spend Saturday morning at the market with your lover, then prepare this picnic together when you get home?

Ratatouille

	1	small eggplant, peeled and thinly sliced
1/2 tbsp	7.5 mL	butter
1/2 tbsp	7.5 mL	olive oil
	1	small zucchini, thinly sliced
	1	onion, thinly sliced
	1	small green pepper, thinly sliced
	1	large tomato, peeled, seeded and cut into eighths
		salt, pepper and fresh basil to taste

Slice the eggplant, place the slices in a bowl and sprinkle with salt. Leave for 30 minutes, then drain.

Heat the butter and olive oil in a skillet. Gently sauté the eggplant, zucchini, onion and green pepper until soft. Add the tomato, salt, pepper and basil and simmer for 10 minutes. Serve hot or cold.

Omelette aux Fines Herbes

1 tsp	5 mL	dried tarragon leaves, marjoram and chives, combined
2 tsp	10 mL	chopped fresh parsley and shallots, combined
	4	eggs
		salt and pepper to taste
1 tsp	5 mL	butter
		cherry tomatoes and sprigs of parsley for garnish

Chop the dried and fresh herbs together. Combine the herbs, eggs, salt and pepper in a bowl. Beat lightly with a fork until the egg white is incorporated.

Heat an omelette pan or small skillet thoroughly. Add the butter. It should sizzle and froth, then turn nut brown, but not burn.

Pour in half of the egg mixture and stir with the flat of a fork until at least half of the mixture is set. Cook until the surface is creamy and the underside is golden. Fold the omelette in half and slide onto a warm plate. Brush with a little butter and garnish with cherry tomatoes and parsley. Repeat with the remaining mixture. Complete your meal with tart fall apples and sharp cheddar cheese.

A Mountain Pass

MENU

AVOCADO AND BACON BITS ON
CRACKED WHEAT BREAD
WATERCRESS SALAD
BANANA BREAD

Nature lovers aren't the only ones to enjoy the privacy of a mountain hike. For your next mountain pass be sure to take along this tempting picnic.

Avocado and Bacon Bits on Cracked Wheat Bread

Homemade Mayonnaise, page 14
4 slices cracked wheat bread
1 avocado, peeled, sliced and sprinkled with lemon juice
2 tbsp 30 mL bacon bits
salt and pepper to taste

Spread mayonnaise on four slices of cracked wheat bread, place several slices of avocado on top and sprinkle with crushed cooked bacon. Season with salt and pepper.

Watercress Salad

1 bunch fresh watercress, trimmed of lower stems
2 spring onions, finely chopped
juice of 1/2 lime
salt and pepper

Toss all ingredients together and serve cold.

Banana Bread

1 cup 250 mL all-purpose flour
1/2 cup 125 mL brown sugar
1/2 tsp 2.5 mL baking powder
1/2 tsp 2.5 mL baking soda
1/2 cup 125 mL shortening
1 tsp 5 mL vanilla extract
juice of 1/2 lemon
2 eggs
3/4 cup 175 mL mashed banana
2 tbsp 30 mL crushed walnuts

Preheat the oven to 350°F (180°C). In a large bowl, sift together the flour, sugar, baking powder and baking soda. Add the shortening, vanilla, lemon juice, eggs and half of the mashed banana. Beat with an electric mixer for 2 minutes. Add the remaining banana, making sure to scrape the bowl. Beat until well combined. Fold in the walnuts. Pour into a large greased loaf pan and bake for 30 to 40 minutes, or until a knife inserted in the middle comes out clean. Cool.

Fireflies and Falling Leaves

MENU

LAMB KABOBS

TABBOULEH
(CRACKED WHEAT SALAD)

PITA BREAD

Warm your hands over the coals of the last barbecue of the year and watch the sparks dance like fireflies. Share this unusual autumn picnic while celebrating nature's change of season.

Lamb Kabobs

1 lb	500 g	lean leg of lamb, cut into 1 in. (2.5 cm) cubes
1/4 cup	60 mL	olive oil
		juice of 1/2 lemon
1 tsp	5 mL	finely chopped fresh mint (half quantity, if dried)
1 tsp	5 mL	finely chopped fresh sage (half quantity, if dried)
1/2 tsp	2.5 mL	dried marjoram
		salt and freshly ground pepper
	1	fresh zucchini, cut into 1 in. (2.5 cm) cubes
	2	large onions, cut into chunks
	2	large tomatoes, cut into chunks

Place the lamb in a marinade of oil, lemon juice, mint, sage, marjoram, salt and pepper. Cover and refrigerate for at least 2 hours. Turn the meat several times in the marinade.

Alternate the lamb, zucchini, onion and tomato on skewers. Brush a hot grill with oil just before putting on the kabobs. Grill for 5 to 7 minutes, turning once. The lamb should be brown on the outside and pink and juicy inside. Serve with a bowl of tabbouleh and pita bread.

Tabbouleh

1/2 cup	125 mL	burghul (cracked wheat)
	1	cucumber, peeled and finely chopped
	2	tomatoes, finely chopped
1/2 cup	125 mL	finely chopped Italian parsley (flat-leaf)
1/2 cup	125 mL	finely chopped onion
		juice of 2 lemons
1/3 cup	75 mL	olive oil
2 tbsp	30 mL	finely chopped fresh mint
		salt and pepper to taste
	4	romaine lettuce leaves

Soak the burghul in cold water for 20 minutes to soften it, then squeeze it dry with your hands. Combine the cracked wheat with the other ingredients and refrigerate. Arrange over the romaine leaves just before serving.

A Lovers' Thanksgiving

MENU

ROAST PHEASANT WITH TRUFFLES
BROWN RICE WITH PINE NUTS
ACORN SQUASH
CHAMPAGNE
PUMPKIN PIE

Celebrate Thanksgiving with your lover. Raise a glass of champagne in honor of love and feast on nature's bountiful harvest.

Roast Pheasant with Truffles

1   hen pheasant, fresh or thawed
1   small can truffles
    salt and pepper
2   bacon slices, cut in halves
1 cup 250 mL   chicken stock

Thinly slice 2 truffles and slide the slices between the skin and the breast meat of the pheasant. Put the bird in a plastic bag and refrigerate for 24 hours.

Preheat oven to 400°F (205°C). Sprinkle the bird with salt and pepper inside and out. Put the bacon strips over the breast. Place the pheasant in a small roasting pan on the top of the stove. Pour in the stock. Partially cover and bring to a boil. Transfer the pan to the bottom rack of the oven. Reduce the heat to 350°F (180°C) and cook for 45 minutes.

Drain off the liquid and reserve for future use. Put the bird, uncovered, back into the oven and broil for 5 to 8 minutes, or until the bacon is well browned. Serve hot, accompanied with brown rice sprinkled with pine nuts, and acorn squash. Enjoy a glass of well-chilled champagne with this picnic.

Acorn Squash

1		medium-sized acorn squash
2 tbsp	30 mL	butter
2 tbsp	30 mL	brown sugar
1 tbsp	15 mL	sherry

Preheat the oven to 350°F (180°C). Cut the squash in halves and remove the seeds and filaments. Combine the butter, sugar and sherry. Spoon the mixture into the squash halves. Place the squash in a small baking dish with a little water. Cover. Bake for 30 to 40 minutes, or until the squash is tender. Serve hot.

Pumpkin Pie

2		eggs, beaten
1-1/2 cups	375 mL	cooked or canned pumpkin
2 cups	500 mL	light cream
1/2 cup	125 mL	honey
1/4 cup	60 mL	brown sugar
1 tsp	5 mL	cinnamon
1/2 tsp	2.5 mL	ground ginger
1/4 tsp	1.25 mL	mace
1/2 tsp	2.5 mL	salt
		juice of 1/2 lemon
		Pie Pastry, for a single-crust pie, page 20

Preheat the oven to 425°F (220°C). Combine all the ingredients, except the pie crust, in blender until smooth. Pour the mixture into the pie shell and bake for 15 minutes. Reduce the heat to 350°F (180°C) and bake for 40 to 50 minutes longer. Serve hot or cold with whipped or ice cream.

For the Bewitching Hour

MENU

PUMPKIN SOUP BAKED IN THE PUMPKIN
SWEET RED AND GREEN PEPPER SALAD
BAKED APPLES

A spell is cast at midnight,
Two lovers softly flee,
While potions and love philters
Are brewed in secrecy.

Sweet magic falls upon the path,
A jack o'lantern is their light,
The lovers drink, and so begins
A secret love feast in the night.

Pumpkin Soup Baked in the Pumpkin

1		small pumpkin, with a solid flat bottom
1 cup	250 mL	crouton cubes
1/2 cup	125 mL	Swiss cheese, grated and firmly packed
1/2 cup	125 mL	Mozzarella cheese, grated and firmly packed
1 cup	250 mL	table cream
1 cup	250 mL	whipping cream
1/2 cup	125 mL	stock (beef, chicken or vegetable)
1 tbsp	15 mL	chopped fresh parsley
		salt and pepper to taste

Preheat the oven to 425°F (220°C). Cut a circular lid out of the top of the pumpkin and set aside. Clean out all the seeds and filaments. Combine the remaining ingredients and fill the pumpkin three-quarters full. Put the lid back on the pumpkin. Wrap the pumpkin in foil, three-quarters of the way up, and place it in a pan of simmering water. Bake for 1-1/2 to 2 hours.

Pre-heat two bowls. Serve the soup hot from the pumpkin, mixing in some of the flesh from the sides of the pumpkin (as much or as little as desired).

Sweet Red and Green Pepper Salad

1		small, firm sweet red pepper, seeded and cut into strips
1		small, firm green pepper, seeded and cut into strips
1		small onion, in thin rings
		parsley
1/2 tbsp	7.5 mL	wine vinegar
1-1/2 tbsp	22.5 mL	sunflower seed oil
1/4 tsp	1.25 mL	dry mustard
1 tsp	5 mL	chopped fresh basil (half quantity, if dried)
1 tsp	5 mL	chopped fresh mint (half quantity, if dried)
		salt and freshly ground pepper to taste

Combine the first 4 ingredients in a salad bowl. Thoroughly mix together the remaining ingredients and pour over the peppers just before serving. This salad may be made in advance and refrigerated until needed.

Baked Apples

2		large tart apples
2 tbsp	30 mL	brown sugar
		dash of cinnamon
1 tsp	5 mL	butter
		heavy cream

Preheat the oven to 375°F (190°C). Leaving the base of the apples intact, remove the cores with a knife or apple corer. To prevent the skins from bursting, peel the skin from the top third of each apple. Fill the apples with brown sugar, cinnamon and butter. Place the apples upright in a baking dish with a bit of water to prevent sticking. Bake for 30 minutes, or until tender. Serve hot, topped with cream, whipped or plain.

Love and the Long-distance Runner

MENU

APPLE JUICE
AVOCADO STUFFED WITH TUNA
CARROT CAKE

Sweating foreheads, aching knees and heavy breathing. It's hard to imagine anything as unromantic as jogging. Unless, of course, you jog with someone else and cheat a little! Convince your lover to join you with promises of a healthy body (possibly), a healthy picnic (definitely) and a little loving (naturally).

Avocado Stuffed with Tuna

1		ripe avocado
		lemon juice
1		small can of tuna fish, drained
2 tbsp	30 mL	finely chopped pickles
2 tbsp	30 mL	finely chopped shallots
1/2 tsp	2.5 mL	capers
1 tbsp	15 mL	chopped fresh parsley
2 tbsp	30 mL	Homemade Mayonnaise, page 14
		juice of 1/2 lemon
		salt and pepper to taste

Slice the avocado in halves and remove the stone. Rub with a little lemon juice to prevent discoloration. Combine the remaining ingredients and fill the avocado halves. Wrap in foil and pack in a box or plastic container, so the avocado doesn't get squashed. Take along a spoon.

Carrot Cake

1 cup	250 mL	flour
1 tsp	5 mL	baking soda
2 tsp	10 mL	baking powder
1/2 tsp	2.5 mL	cinnamon
		dash of salt
1-1/2 cups	375 mL	grated carrots
3/4 cup	175 mL	vegetable oil or butter
3/4 cup	175 mL	honey
		juice of 1/2 lemon
2		eggs, beaten
2 tbsp	30 mL	crushed walnuts or almond slivers

Preheat the oven to 350°F (180°C). Combine all the dry ingredients, then stir in the carrots, oil, honey, lemon juice, eggs and nuts. Mix well. Pour into a greased baking pan and bake for 45 minutes, or until a knife inserted in the center comes out clean. Cool.

72

Pour les Amants Minceurs

MENU

SPINACH NOODLES WITH CLAM SAUCE
DRY WHITE WINE
FRESH FRUIT SALAD

We're the first to admit that love and food go together and so, "pour les amants minceurs", who may be watching calories, although they wish they didn't have to, we offer a light seafood pasta to give you the illusion that you are denying yourselves nothing.

Spinach Noodles with Clam Sauce

1 tbsp	15 mL	butter
3/4 cup	175 mL	dry white wine
1 tbsp	15 mL	finely chopped fresh parsley
1 tsp	5 mL	finely chopped fresh basil
1 tsp	5 mL	finely chopped fresh oregano
	18	clams in their shells
		(the shells should be whole and tightly closed)
	1	onion, finely chopped
	1	garlic clove, finely chopped
1 tbsp	15 mL	finely chopped shallots
1 tsp	5 mL	butter
1 tsp	5 mL	flour
1 tbsp	15 mL	cold water
2 tbsp	30 mL	table cream
		white pepper to taste
1/4 lb	125 g	fine spinach noodles
4 cups	1 L	water
1 tbsp	15 mL	vegetable oil
		butter

In a large pot combine the 1 tbsp (15 mL) butter, wine, parsley, basil and oregano. Bring to a boil. Add the clams and cover. Reduce the heat and simmer, shaking the pot once or twice until all the clams have opened. Remove the clams from the broth and reserve the broth. Discard any unopened shells. Remove the clams from their shells and reserve.

In a skillet, fry the onion, garlic and shallots until transparent in the 1 tsp (5 mL) of butter. Pour in the clam broth, bring to a boil and boil for 2 to 3 minutes.

Combine the flour and the 1 tbsp (15 mL) of cold water in a small closed container and shake until blended. Stir the flour mixture vigorously into the hot clam broth. Add the clams, cream and white pepper. Taste. Add salt only if necessary. Simmer for 2 to 3 minutes.

Meanwhile, place the spinach noodles in 4 cups (1 L) boiling salted water, with the oil to prevent stickiness. Cook for about 7 minutes, or until the pasta is *al dente* (tender but firm). Drain. Mix in a bit of butter. Pour the hot clam sauce over the pasta and serve immediately. Delicious with a chilled bottle of dry white wine.

Fresh Fruit Salad

1   apple, peeled, cored and cut into eighths
1   orange, peeled and sectioned
1   banana, cut into thin slices
1   pear, peeled, cored and cut into eighths
1   bunch of green grapes
    seeds from 1 pomegranate
1   kiwi fruit, peeled and cut into thin slices
    juice of 1 lemon
    juice of 1/2 lime
    juice of 1 orange
    fruit sugar (optional)

Combine the fruit in two fruit bowls. Pour the lemon, lime and orange juice over the fruit and sprinkle with fruit sugar. Serve cold.

For Midnight Lovers

MENU

ARTICHOKES
GRILLED SCAMPI WITH GARLIC SAUCE
WHITE WINE OR CHAMPAGNE
PEARS IN CHAMPAGNE

This elegant menu is reserved for midnight lovers. The sensual artichoke makes a seductive starter for a late-night picnic in front of the fireplace. As you grill your scampi, share a glass of champagne and celebrate the magic of the night.

Artichokes

2		medium-sized globe artichokes
1		lemon
1		bay leaf
1/2 tsp	2.5 mL	sea salt
		Homemade Mayonnaise, page 14, or
		Vinaigrette Dressing, page 33

Follow the instructions on page 47 for preparing the artichokes. Cook for 30-40 minutes or until a lower leaf pulls out easily and the meat at the base of the leaf is tender.

Remove the artichokes from the boiling water and drain them upside down. Serve warm. Pluck the leaves off, one by one. Dip the base of the leaf in homemade mayonnaise or vinaigrette dressing, then scrape the flesh off with your teeth. At the bottom of the artichoke, you will find the heart, just beneath the hairy choke. With your fingers, remove the choke and eat the heart.

Grilled Scampi with Garlic Sauce

2		shallots, finely chopped
2		large garlic cloves, finely chopped
2 tbsp	30 mL	finely chopped fresh parsley
		salt and freshly ground pepper to taste
1/4 cup	60 mL	butter
8		jumbo scampi, fresh or thawed

Combine all the ingredients, except the scampi, in a saucepan and heat gently while you cook the scampi. Place the scampi, underside down, on a greased grill over the fireplace. Grill for 5 minutes, or until done. Dip the flesh into the hot garlic sauce and enjoy with a well-chilled white wine or champagne left over from preparing the dessert.

He brought me to the banqueting house,
and his banner over me was love.
THE SONG OF SOLOMON

Pears in Champagne

1 cup	250 mL	champagne
		juice of 1 lemon
1/2 cup	125 mL	sugar
	2	firm pears, peeled, left whole with stems attached

Combine the champagne, lemon juice and sugar in a saucepan. Bring to a boil, stirring to make sure the sugar is completely dissolved. Reduce to medium heat. Place the peeled pears in the champagne mixture, cover and cook for 15 to 20 minutes, or until the pears are slightly tender. Do not overcook the pears or they will become mushy.

Remove the pears, boil the liquid and rapidly reduce by half. Pour the liquid over the pears, cool to room temperature, then refrigerate for several hours. The liquid will become syrupy with refrigeration. Spoon the syrup over the pears before serving.

No spring, nor summer beauty hath such grace,
As I have seen in one autumnal face.
JOHN DONNE

Autumn Sonata

MENU

CREAM OF ZUCCHINI SOUP
BAKED EGGPLANT WITH CHEESE AND TOMATO

Before the last flourish of color is covered by a blanket of snow, decorate your table for two with fall leaves, light a candle, and enjoy autumn's finale.

Cream of Zucchini Soup

2 cups	500 mL	chicken stock
	1 or 2	zucchini, sliced into 1/2 in. (1 cm) pieces
	1	large onion, chopped
	1	small tomato, cubed
1 tsp	5 mL	crushed coriander seeds
		salt and freshly ground pepper
1/4 cup	60 mL	heavy cream

Bring the chicken stock to a boil, add the zucchini, onion, tomato, coriander, salt and pepper and simmer for 20 minutes. Mix in a blender until smooth, adding the cream. Serve hot or cold.

Baked Eggplant with Cheese and Tomato

	1	small eggplant, cut into 8 slices 1/2 in. (1 cm) wide
2 tbsp	30 mL	vegetable oil
		flour
	1	large tomato, cut into 8 slices
		salt and pepper to taste
	4	slices of Mozzarella cheese, cut in halves
	4	slices of Swiss cheese, cut in halves

Sprinkle salt over the eggplant and set aside for 30 minutes. Drain and pat dry.

Heat the oil in a skillet. Dust the eggplant slices with flour and fry over medium heat for 3 to 5 minutes on each side, until the eggplant is tender.

Top each piece of eggplant with a slice of tomato and season with salt and pepper. Add the slices of Mozzarella and Swiss cheese. Cover and cook until all the cheese has melted. Serve hot.

Chestnuts Roasting
on an Open Fire

A Night with the Czar

MENU

VODKA

RUSSIAN EGGS

STEAK TARTARE

PUMPERNICKEL BREAD

BLACK RUSSIAN TEA OR SIMPLY A BLACK RUSSIAN

Imagine yourself in the icy wasteland of Russia. The czar welcomes you to his hideaway, with a glass of vodka and a huge animal fur to keep you warm, and invites you to share a royal picnic. A far-fetched fantasy? When the winter winds howl, Russia doesn't seem all that far away.

Russian Eggs

4		hard-boiled eggs
1/4 cup	60 mL	Homemade Mayonnaise, page 14
1 tbsp	15 mL	chili sauce
1 tsp	5 mL	chopped fresh chives
		pinch of cayenne pepper
		juice of 1/2 lemon
		dash of paprika

Shell the eggs and cut them in halves. Combine the mayonnaise, chili sauce, chives, cayenne pepper and lemon juice and spread over the eggs. Sprinkle with paprika and serve cold.

Steak Tartare

1/2 lb	250 g	top sirloin, ground
	1	onion, finely chopped
1 tsp	5 mL	Dijon mustard
1 tsp	5 mL	capers
1 tbsp	15 mL	chopped fresh parsley
		salt and freshly ground pepper
		cognac
	2	egg yolks

Combine the meat, onion, mustard, capers, parsley, salt and lots of pepper. Sprinkle with cognac. Make two patties, with a slight depression in the center of each. Place the egg yolk in this well. Serve at room temperature.

Steak tartare may also be spread on pumpernickel bread and topped with black lumpfish or caviar. (If you think you'll need a bit of courage to try steak tartare, skip the tea and mix up a Black Russian!)

Black Russian

1/3	of a glass of Kahlua
2/3	of a glass of vodka
	ice

Combine the vodka and Kahlua and pour over ice in a short or old-fashioned glass.

Rasputin's Retreat

MENU

CREAM OF CHESTNUT SOUP
UNSHUCKED OYSTERS
CHAMPAGNE
CHOCOLATE MOUSSE WITH MANDARIN ORANGES

Deep in the cellar of the czar's castle, Rasputin prepares his love philters. Devil or genius, he will work his magic on the czarina and perhaps even on you.

Cream of Chestnut Soup

1/2 lb	250 g	fresh chestnuts
1 tbsp	15 mL	butter
	1	onion, finely chopped
	1	garlic clove, finely chopped
	1	bay leaf
		freshly ground pepper, salt, thyme and nutmeg to taste
2 cups	500 mL	chicken stock
1 tbsp	15 mL	sherry
2 tbsp	30 mL	heavy cream

To shell the chestnuts, cut a cross on the flat side of each nut with a sharp knife. Plunge the nuts into a pot of boiling water and bring to a boil again for 1 minute. Remove from the heat. Using a slotted spoon, lift out the chestnuts 2 or 3 at a time. (Set aside difficult chestnuts and reboil for another minute.) Peel off both the outer and inner skins.

Chop the chestnuts into quarters. Heat the butter in a skillet and fry the onion and garlic until transparent. Add the chestnuts along with the bay leaf, pepper, salt, thyme and nutmeg and cook over low heat for 3 to 4 minutes. Add the stock and bring to a boil. Reduce to a simmer and pour in the sherry. Continue cooking for about 20 minutes, or until the chestnuts are soft. Pour the mixture into a blender along with the cream and blend until smooth. Serve hot.

Unshucked Oysters

2	dozen oysters in their shells
2	limes, cut in halves

Wash the oysters under cold water and scrub well. To open the shells, hold the broad side of the oyster with one hand, insert a strong knife (preferably an oyster knife) between the shells, twist and pry apart. Squeeze lime juice over the oyster flesh and serve in the shell. Accompany with a glass of chilled champagne.

Chocolate Mousse with Mandarin Oranges

	2	squares semi-sweet baking chocolate
2 tbsp	30 mL	milk
1 tbsp	15 mL	Cointreau
	2	egg yolks
1-1/2 tbsp	22.5 mL	unsalted butter, softened
	3	egg whites
	1	mandarin orange, peeled and sectioned

Place the chocolate, milk and Cointreau in a small saucepan. Cover and heat just to a boil. Remove from the heat at once and stir until smooth. Thoroughly incorporate the egg yolks, one at a time, then add the butter, a little at a time, stirring until smooth. Set aside. (To avoid watery mousse, be sure to prepare this chocolate mixture first.)

Whip the egg whites (preferably in a copper bowl) into soft peaks. Gently fold the chocolate mixture into the whites. Do not overfold or the mousse will become too liquid. Pour into glass or china cups and chill for at least 2 hours. Serve topped with sections of mandarin orange.

There will be work for questing hands
And fingers play their part
Exploring those mysterious lands
Where Cupid bathes his burning dart.
OVID

Coureurs de Bois

MENU

CREAM OF VEGETABLE SOUP

PÂTÉ AUX FINES HERBES

BAGUETTE
(FRENCH BREAD)

DRY RED WINE

KNAPSACK NIBBLES

History tells us that the coureurs de bois travelled many lonely days and nights on snowshoes to deliver a message to a loved one. Make your own history with a cross-country ski trek. Share the snowy trails and this tasty and hearty picnic with your lover.

Cream of Vegetable Soup

1		large onion, chopped
1		large garlic clove, chopped
1		celery stalk, chopped
1/2 cup	125 mL	chopped cabbage
1		large tomato, peeled, seeded and chopped
1/4 cup	60 mL	chopped fresh parsley
1		carrot, chopped
1-1/2 cups	375 mL	chicken broth
1		bay leaf, crushed
1 tsp	5 mL	finely chopped fresh basil (half quantity, if dried)
1 tsp	5 mL	finely chopped fresh thyme (half quantity, if dried)
1 tsp	5 mL	finely chopped fresh chives (half quantity, if dried)
		salt and pepper to taste
2 tbsp	30 mL	sour cream

Over medium heat, cook all the ingredients, except the sour cream, for 20 minutes, or until tender. Mix in a blender until smooth, adding the sour cream. Serve hot or cold. (For cold soup, additional salt and pepper may be required.)

Pâté aux Fines Herbes

1/2 lb	250 g	livers (chicken, beef or calf), sliced
2 tbsp	30 mL	finely chopped shallots
1 tbsp	15 mL	finely chopped parsley
1 tbsp	15 mL	butter
1/2 tbsp	7.5 mL	oil
		salt and pepper to taste
1 tbsp	15 mL	cognac
1 tbsp	15 mL	stock (chicken or beef)
1 tbsp	15 mL	heavy cream
1/3 cup	75 mL	butter, softened
2 tbsp	30 mL	finely chopped fresh basil, thyme and tarragon, combined (half quantity, if dried)
2 tbsp	30 mL	clarified butter

Over medium heat sauté the livers, shallots and parsley in the 1 tbsp (15 mL) butter and the oil until the livers are browned on the outside but slightly pink in the center. Season with salt and pepper. Sprinkle the livers with cognac, light with a match and shake the pan until the flame goes out. Transfer to a blender. Add the stock and cream and blend until smooth. Set aside to cool completely.

Meanwhile, cream the 1/3 cup (75 mL) butter with the basil, thyme and tarragon. Mix thoroughly with the cooled liver purée. Pour into a 1-1/2 cup (375 mL) pâté mold or into individual ramekins. Top with the clarified butter and refrigerate.

Ideally the pâté should age for a week, but it may be eaten as early as 12 hours after preparation. Serve cold accompanied by a baguette and a wine-skin filled with dry red wine.

Knapsack Nibbles

1/4 cup   60 mL   raisins
1/4 cup   60 mL   mixed nuts
1/4 cup   60 mL   chopped dried apricots
1/4 cup   60 mL   dark chocolate, cut into pieces

Combine the ingredients and store in a plastic bag. These nibbles should give you all the energy necessary to make angels in the snow.

Après-Ski Love

MENU

HOT APPLE CIDER DRINK
CREAM OF CAULIFLOWER SOUP
WIENER SCHNITZEL
RICE OR EGG NOODLES
RED CABBAGE

Whether you spend an energetic day on the slopes or decide to skip the skiing altogether, you'll enjoy this creamy homemade soup followed by Wiener Schnitzel and red cabbage. Start with spicy hot cider to take off the chill.

Hot Apple Cider Drink

4 cups	1 L	apple cider
	4	whole cloves
	1	cinnamon stick
	4	whole allspice
1/4 cup	60 mL	calvados or brandy

Combine the ingredients in a saucepan and bring to a boil. Cover and simmer for 10 minutes. Strain the cider to remove the spices and serve hot.

Cream of Cauliflower Soup

	1	small cauliflower, broken into florets
	1	large onion, chopped
	1	garlic clove, chopped
2 cups	500 mL	chicken stock
	1	bay leaf, crushed
		salt and white pepper to taste
		dash of cayenne pepper
1/4 cup	60 mL	heavy cream

Cook all the ingredients, except the cream, over medium heat for 20 minutes, or until the cauliflower is tender. Transfer to a blender and blend until smooth, adding the cream. Serve hot.

Wiener Schnitzel

		2	large, thin veal cutlets
2 tbsp	30 mL		flour
		1	egg, beaten
			salt and pepper
2 tbsp	30 mL		bread crumbs
1 tbsp	15 mL		butter
1 tbsp	15 mL		vegetable oil
			lemon juice

To prevent the meat from curling during cooking, have your butcher remove the membrane from the cutlets. Pound the cutlets until they become very thin or ask your butcher to do this. Dust them with flour, then dip them into the beaten egg seasoned with salt and pepper. Roll the cutlets in the bread crumbs until they are completely coated.

Heat the butter and oil in a skillet over medium heat. When very hot, add the cutlets and cook for 3 to 4 minutes on each side. Sprinkle with lemon juice and serve with rice or egg noodles and red cabbage.

Red Cabbage

		1/2	onion, chopped
1 tsp	5 mL		butter
1-1/2 cups	375 mL		shredded red cabbage
2 tbsp	30 mL		water
1-1/2 tbsp	22.5 mL		vinegar
1 tbsp	15 mL		sugar
1 tsp	5 mL		salt

Over medium heat, brown the onions in the butter. Add the red cabbage and sauté for 2 to 3 minutes. Pour in the water and vinegar. Add the sugar and salt and bring to a boil. Immediately reduce to simmer, cover and cook for 20 to 30 minutes. Taste and add more sugar or vinegar as desired. Serve hot.

Land of the Midnight Sun

MENU

ARCTIC SALAD
LIVER FLAMED WITH COGNAC
ICE CREAM WITH MAPLE SYRUP

Few of us will witness the beauty of the sun reflecting on an iceberg at midnight or the flight of a ptarmigan. But you and your lover can experience a taste of the northland. Curl up in front of a roaring fire and try this delicious arctic feast.

Arctic Salad

	1	small can arctic char or salmon
2 tbsp	30 mL	Homemade Mayonnaise, page 14
	1/2	stalk celery, chopped
	2	green onions, finely chopped
1 tbsp	15 mL	chopped fresh parsley
1 tsp	5 mL	chopped fresh dill (half quantity, if dried)
1 tsp	5 mL	capers
		salt and pepper to taste
		iceberg lettuce leaves for garnish

Combine all the ingredients and garnish with the lettuce leaves.

Liver Flamed with Cognac

	1	onion, in thin rings
1/4 cup	60 mL	finely chopped shallots
1 tbsp	15 mL	butter
	2	bacon slices, chopped
1/2 lb	250 g	baby beef liver, cut into bite-sized pieces
1/2 cup	125 mL	coarsely chopped parsley
		salt and freshly ground pepper
1 tbsp	15 mL	cognac
1 tbsp	15 mL	heavy cream
		rice or egg noodles

Over medium heat, sauté the onion and shallots in the butter until transparent. Add the bacon and cook for 3 to 4 minutes. Add the liver and cook for 5 minutes, turning once. Mix in the parsley, salt and lots of pepper and cook for 3 minutes more. Pour cognac over the liver and light with a match. Shake the skillet until the flame goes out. Mix in the cream and serve warm over rice or egg noodles.

A bright torch, and a casement ope at night
To let the warm love in!
JOHN KEATS

To Spice Up Your Love Life

MENU

CURRIED SHRIMP WITH RICE

FRIED CAULIFLOWER

MANGO WITH ICE CREAM

According to legend, the spices used in curries are renowned for their romantic properties. Combined with the sensuous smoothness of tropical mango, these curried shrimp are certain to add spice to your love life.

Curried Shrimp with Rice

1/2 lb	250 g	dessicated coconut
2 cups	500 mL	hot water
	1	onion, finely chopped
	1	garlic clove, finely chopped
2 tbsp	30 mL	vegetable oil
	1	cinnamon stick
	2	cloves
1 tsp	5 mL	cumin seeds
	2	cardamom pods
	1	bay leaf
	1	tomato, peeled and chopped
		dash of turmeric
1 tsp	5 mL	ginger
1 tsp	5 mL	curry powder
1 tsp	5 mL	salt
		dash of cayenne pepper
1/2 lb	250 g	fresh, medium-sized shrimp, shelled
		rice

Soak the dessicated coconut in the hot water for 30 minutes to make coconut milk. Over medium heat, fry the onion and garlic in the oil with the cinnamon stick, cloves, cumin seed, cardamom pods and bay leaf, until the onion is translucent. Add the tomato, turmeric, ginger, curry powder, salt and cayenne pepper and cook for 2 to 3 minutes. Add the shrimp.

Pour 1 cup (250 mL) of the coconut milk into the shrimp mixture. Bring to a boil, then simmer for 30 minutes. Add 2 tbsp (30 mL) of the moist dessicated coconut to thicken. Serve hot over bed of rice.

Variety's the very spice of life.
WILLIAM COWPER

Fried Cauliflower

1/4 cup	60 mL	flour
1/2 tsp	2.5 mL	baking powder
1/4 tsp	1.25 mL	salt
3 tbsp	45 mL	milk
1/4 tsp	1.25 mL	cumin seeds
		pinch of cayenne pepper
		freshly ground pepper to taste
1 tsp	5 mL	vegetable oil
	1/2	small cauliflower, broken into florets
1/4 cup	60 mL	vegetable oil

Combine all the ingredients, except the last 2, in a blender. Blend for 1 minute, scraping the sides of the blender bowl occasionally. Steam the cauliflower until tender-crisp. Be careful not to overcook the vegetable or it will become mushy. Cool.

Dip the cauliflower pieces into the batter, thinly coating them. Heat the 1/4 cup (60 mL) oil in a frying pan and fry the florets for 3 to 4 minutes over medium heat, turning them frequently. When they are golden brown, place the florets on a paper towel to drain. Serve hot.

Mango with Ice Cream

1	ripe mango or canned mango
	ice cream
	twist of lemon

Peel the mango and cut bite-sized pieces from around the stone. (As it is somewhat messy and difficult to cut up a ripe mango, you might want to resort to canned mango.) Serve over ice cream with a twist of lemon.

A Night in the Tatra Mountains

MENU

SAUERKRAUT SOUP
RYE BREAD
BEER
APPLE PIE

In central Europe a hearty bowlful of sauerkraut soup is traditionally served after a day of skiing or a night of dancing. (A pot of this steaming soup, rich in sauerkraut, sausage, mushrooms and sour cream, will also do wonders for a hangover!)

Sauerkraut Soup

3/4 cup	175 mL	sauerkraut
2 cups	500 mL	water
1 tsp	5 mL	sugar
1 tbsp	15 mL	dried mushrooms
1 tbsp	15 mL	fresh mushrooms, chopped
	1	smoked European sausage (any kind, except Polish sausage)
2 tbsp	30 mL	sour cream
		salt and pepper to taste

Combine the sauerkraut and water in a pot and bring to a boil. Add the sugar and continue to boil over medium heat for 30 minutes.

While the sauerkraut is cooking, soak the dried mushrooms in warm water for 30 minutes. Drain. Add the soaked mushrooms to the sauerkraut along with the fresh mushrooms and sausage. Continue to cook for 20 minutes longer. You may wish to add more water, if the liquid starts to evaporate.

Remove the sausage, cut it into bite-sized pieces and return it to the soup. Stir in the sour cream. Season with salt and pepper. Serve hot with rye bread and a frothy mug of beer.

Apple Pie

1 tbsp	15 mL	fine bread crumbs
	4 - 6	apples, peeled, cored and cut into eighths
2 tbsp	30 mL	sugar
		juice of 1/2 lemon
		dash of vanilla
		butter
		Pie Pastry, for a double-crust pie, page 20
		cream

Preheat the oven to 350°F (180°C). Sprinkle the bread crumbs on the bottom of the uncooked pie shell. Place the sliced apples over the bread crumbs and top with the sugar, lemon juice, vanilla and a dot of butter. Cover with the top pie pastry. Pierce the top of the pie with a fork and brush it with cream. Cook for 40 minutes or until golden. Serve hot or cold.

From Italy with Love

MENU

SPAGHETTI WITH HOMEMADE MEAT SAUCE
CAESAR SALAD
DRY RED ITALIAN WINE

Shall we let you in on a well-known secret? Forget the fancy, unpronouncable delicacies. Instead, try a little love, Italian-style. A pot of spaghetti with homemade meat sauce, a bottle of Italian red wine, a tangy salad and, of course, a siesta. It's been tested successfully for centuries.

Spaghetti with Homemade Meat Sauce

	1	large onion, cut into thin rings
	1	large garlic clove, finely chopped
1 tbsp	15 mL	oil
1/2 lb	250 g	lean minced beef
	1	bay leaf
1/2 tsp	2.5 mL	dried basil
1/2 tsp	2.5 mL	dried oregano
1/4 tsp	1.25 mL	crushed dried red chilies
1/2 tsp	2.5 mL	salt
1/2 tsp	2.5 mL	freshly ground pepper
10 oz	284 mL	stewed tomatoes
5-1/2 oz	156 mL	tomato paste
1/4 cup	60 mL	red wine
1/2 cup	125 mL	cubed green peppers
1/2 cup	125 mL	coarsely chopped mushrooms
1/4 lb	125 g	thin spaghetti noodles
4 cups	1 L	water, salted
1 tbsp	15 mL	oil
		butter

Over medium heat, fry the onion and the garlic in the oil until the onion is transparent. Mix in the meat, bay leaf, basil, oregano, chilies, salt and pepper. Brown for 15 minutes. Stir in the tomatoes, tomato paste and the wine. Simmer for one hour, stirring occasionally. Add the green peppers and mushrooms and simmer for 15 minutes or until the vegetables are slightly tender.

While the sauce is cooking, place the noodles in the boiling salted water, with the oil to prevent stickiness. Cook for about 7 minutes or until the pasta is *al dente* (tender but firm). Drain. Mix in a nut of butter and serve hot, topped with meat sauce.

Caesar Salad

		romaine lettuce for 2
1/2 tsp	2.5 mL	salt
		freshly ground pepper to taste
1		garlic clove, finely chopped
1/4 tsp	1.25 mL	dry mustard
1 tsp	5 mL	Worcestershire sauce
1		egg, cooked for 10 seconds in rapidly boiling water
		juice of 1/2 lemon
1 tbsp	15 mL	vegetable oil
1/3 cup	75 mL	Parmesan cheese
6		anchovy filets, cut up
10		garlic croutons

Tear the chilled romaine lettuce into bite-sized pieces and place in a salad bowl. Add the salt, pepper, garlic, mustard, Worcestershire sauce and toss.

Break the egg onto the lettuce, add the lemon juice and oil and toss again until the lettuce leaves are well coated. Toss in the cheese, anchovies and croutons. Serve immediately.

Memories of Mexico

MENU

GUACAMOLE
TORTILLA CHIPS
CHILI
GARLIC BREAD

When you've hung up your skates for the day, sit by the fire and think of Mexico. Warmth and sun will come flooding back to you with your first taste of this smooth guacamole and spicy chili.

Guacamole

	1	ripe avocado
	1	small tomato, peeled, seeded and cut up
		juice of 1/2 lemon
1/4 cup	60 mL	finely chopped onion
1/2 tsp	2.5 mL	crushed coriander
	1	small garlic clove, crushed
1/2 tsp	2.5 mL	chili powder or crushed chilies

Combine all the ingredients in a blender and purée until smooth. Serve with tortilla chips.

Chili

1/2 lb	250 g	ground beef
	1	onion, finely chopped
	1	garlic clove, finely chopped
2 tbsp	30 mL	vegetable oil
10 oz	284 mL	stewed tomatoes
5-1/2 oz	156 mL	tomato paste
1/2 tsp	2.5 mL	chili powder
1 tsp	5 mL	Worcestershire sauce
1 tsp	5 mL	salt
1 tsp	5 mL	freshly ground pepper
		dash of cayenne pepper
	1/2	green pepper, coarsely chopped
1/4 lb	125 g	coarsely chopped mushrooms
10 oz	284 mL	kidney beans

Brown the meat, onion and garlic in the oil. Add the stewed tomatoes, tomato paste, chili powder, Worcestershire sauce, salt, pepper and cayenne pepper. Bring to a boil, then simmer for 30 minutes. Add the green pepper, mushrooms and kidney beans and continue to simmer for another 30 minutes, stirring occasionally. Serve hot with warm garlic bread.

For the Perfect Midnight Picnic

MENU

ESCARGOTS AND GARLIC BUTTER SAUCE
FRENCH BREAD
FRENCH OR CALIFORNIA CHABLIS
LEMON MOUSSE WITH RASPBERRY SAUCE

There are some who vow that piping hot escargots smothered in bubbly garlic sauce and a bottle of well-chilled chablis are the secret ingredients for seduction. Why not try these delectable little snails and see for yourself.

Escargots and Garlic Butter Sauce

	2	shallots, finely chopped
	2	large garlic cloves, finely chopped
2 tbsp	30 mL	finely chopped fresh parsley
		salt and freshly ground pepper to taste
1/4 cup	60 mL	butter, softened
	24	canned snails
	24	escargot shells

Preheat the oven to 400°F (205°C). Cream the shallots, garlic, parsley, salt and pepper into the butter until smooth.

Wash the snails and shells in cold water and drain. Place a bit of the garlic butter mixture in the bottom of each shell. Add the snail and fill the shell with more garlic butter. Place the shells open side up in a baking dish and bake for 6 to 8 minutes. (If you don't have any escargot shells, simply bake the snails in the garlic butter and serve in a preheated dish.) Serve hot with crusty French bread to soak up the garlic butter. Accompany with a well-chilled chablis.

Lemon Mousse with Raspberry Sauce

	2	egg yolks
1/4 cup	60 mL	sugar
		juice and grated rind of 1 lemon
	2	egg whites
1/2 cup	125 mL	whipping cream
		Raspberry Sauce, see below
	2	mint leaves for garnish

Beat the egg yolks and sugar with an electric mixer or hand beater until thick. Add the lemon juice and rind. Transfer the mixture to the top of a double boiler and cook over simmering water, stirring constantly, for about 4 minutes, or until the mixture is thick. Cool.

Whip the egg whites until soft peaks form and beat the whipping cream until stiff. Fold together and then fold into the egg mixture. Pour into 2 serving dishes and chill. Spoon raspberry sauce over the mousse just before serving and top with a mint leaf.

106

Raspberry Sauce

1/2 cup   125 mL   frozen raspberries, thawed
2 tbsp   30 mL   sugar
                  juice of 1/2 lemon

Cook the raspberries, sugar and lemon juice over medium heat for several minutes until the sugar is dissolved. Mash the cooked raspberries and liquid through a sieve to remove the seeds. Cool.

The iron tongue of midnight hath told twelve;
Lovers, to bed.
WILLIAM SHAKESPEARE

107

And for the Morning After

MENU

FRESHLY SQUEEZED ORANGE JUICE
EGGS FLORENTINE
BROWN TOAST WITH ROSE HIP JELLY
COFFEE

Celebrate a winter's morning by stealing a few loving
moments at the break of the day. Greet your lover with
a wine-glass full of freshly squeezed orange juice followed by an elegant breakfast.

Eggs Florentine

4 cups	1 L	fresh spinach leaves, packed
1 tsp	5 mL	butter
1 tsp	5 mL	oil
		pinch of nutmeg
		salt and freshly ground pepper
	4	eggs
2 tbsp	30 mL	Parmesan cheese, grated
3/4 cup	175 mL	Béchamel Sauce, page 28

Preheat the oven to 375°F (190°C). Wash the spinach leaves and drain lightly. There should be a little moisture on the leaves.

Heat the butter and the oil in a large skillet. Add the spinach, cover and cook over medium heat for 3 to 5 minutes, or until the leaves are tender. Stir, season with nutmeg, salt and pepper. Transfer the spinach to a lightly greased baking dish. Make 4 wells in the spinach and carefully crack 1 egg into each of these wells. Sprinkle with the cheese and top with béchamel sauce. Bake in the oven for 10 to 12 minutes. Serve hot.

Rose Hip Jelly

2 cups	500 mL	rose hips
		water
		sugar

If you're lucky enough to have found love in the summer (and smart enough to have thought ahead), you can prepare this delicious jelly in early fall and surprise your lover on a winter morning. (Or you can cheat a little and buy some rose hip jelly.)

Wash and pat dry the rose hips. Cut in halves lengthwise and place in a pan with just enough water to cover the first layer of rose hips. Cover and cook over medium heat until the rose hips become tender. This will take at least 15 minutes. Turn the rose hips often and add additional water to prevent them from sticking or burning. Strain through a jelly bag and discard the rose hips.

Boil the liquid and reduce by a quarter. Measure the liquid and add to it the same quantity of sugar. Boil. To test if the jelly is ready, place a spoonful of liquid on a plate to see if it sets well. Bottle the liquid in hot sterilized jars. Delicious on crisp brown toast with freshly brewed coffee.

A Lovers' Christmas

MENU

CUCUMBER SALAD
DUCKLING WITH PLUMS AND GRAPES
BROWN RICE
DRY RED OR WHITE WINE
FLAMING CRÊPES

Mistletoe and magic. A Christmas celebration of love.
Light the candles, blow a kiss to Jack Frost and present
your lover with this festive feast.

Cucumber Salad

	1	medium-sized cucumber, peeled
1 tbsp	15 mL	vinegar
1 tbsp	15 mL	sugar
1 tbsp	15 mL	chopped fresh parsley
		dash of cayenne pepper

Slice the peeled cucumber into paper thin slices. Sprinkle with salt and set aside for 30 minutes. Drain.

Combine the cucumber with the remaining ingredients and chill. Serve cold.

Duckling with Plums and Grapes

4 lb	1.8 kg	duckling, fresh or thawed
		salt and pepper
	10	firm plums, cut in halves and pitted
	12	green grapes
1 tsp	5 mL	butter
2 tbsp	30 mL	honey
		juice of 1/2 lemon

Preheat the oven to 375°F (190°C). Remove the neck and bag of innards from the cavity of the duckling and reserve for soup. Wash, dry, salt and pepper the duckling inside and out. Stuff the cavity with 10 plum halves and 6 grapes. Secure with string or skewers.

Place the duckling in a small roasting pan and cook, uncovered, for 1 hour and 15 minutes. Baste often with the juices from the fruit and the duckling fat. Broil for 3 minutes for added color and crispness. Remove from the oven and discard the fruit stuffing.

In a saucepan, combine the butter, honey, lemon juice and the remaining fruit. Cook over low heat for 5 minutes, or until the fruit is slightly tender. Garnish the duckling with honeyed plums and grapes and serve with brown rice. Accompany with either a dry red or white wine.

Flaming Crêpes

	1	egg
1/2 cup	125 mL	flour
2 tsp	10 mL	sugar
1/2 cup	125 mL	milk
2 tbsp	30 mL	water
2 tsp	10 mL	melted butter
1 tsp	5 mL	grated lemon rind
1 tsp	5 mL	grated orange rind
3 tbsp	45 mL	unsalted butter, melted
1 tbsp	15 mL	Cointreau
		juice of 1/2 lemon
		icing sugar

Combine the egg, flour, sugar, milk, water, the 2 tsp (10 mL) butter and lemon and orange rind in a blender. Blend until smooth.

Place a small skillet or crêpe pan over medium to high heat. When the pan is hot, brush with a little butter. When bubbling, pour in approximately 2 tbsp (30 mL) of the crêpe batter. Remove from the heat and tilt the pan in all directions to spread the batter thinly over the surface of the pan. Return to heat and cook for 2 to 3 minutes, or until the bottom of the crêpe is golden brown. Turn and brown the other side for a few seconds. Set aside in a warm oven. Brush the hot pan with more butter before making another crêpe. The batter will yield 4 to 6 crêpes, depending on whether the first ones turn out.

Fold the crêpes into halves and then into quarters. Add more butter to the crêpe pan. When bubbling, place the folded crêpes in the pan. Sprinkle the Cointreau over the crêpes and light it with a match. Shake the pan until all the flames have gone out. Sprinkle the crêpes with the lemon juice and icing sugar and serve immediately.

Ah, my Beloved, fill the cup that clears
To-day of past Regrets and future Fears
THE RUBÁIYÁT OF OMAR KHAYYÁM

CHERRY
BLOSSOMS

After the Last Roll in the Snow

MENU

HEARTY ONION SOUP
CIDER OR BEER
EGG SALAD SANDWICH TOPPED WITH CAVIAR

Before the spring sun melts the cornsnow, enjoy a last ski outing or toboggan ride and then come home to a hot homemade soup.

114

Hearty Onion Soup

	3	onions, in thin rings
	1	garlic clove, finely chopped
1 tsp	5 mL	butter
		salt and freshly ground pepper
	1	can beef consommé
	1/2	can water
		dash of Worcestershire sauce
1 tbsp	15 mL	cognac
	2	slices of French bread
	2	slices of Swiss cheese
	2	slices of Mozzarella cheese

Fry the onions and garlic in the butter until golden. Season with salt and lots of pepper. Pour in the consommé, water, Worcestershire sauce and cognac. Bring to a boil then simmer for 1 hour.

Top each slice of French bread with 1 slice of Swiss cheese and 1 slice of Mozzarella. Pour the soup into oven-proof bowls, float the bread and cheese on top and broil until the cheese is bubbly and slightly brown. Serve immediately, taking care not to get burned by the bowl. Accompany with cider or beer.

Egg Salad Sandwich Topped with Caviar

	2	hard-boiled eggs, finely chopped
2 tbsp	30 mL	Homemade Mayonnaise, page 14
1 tbsp	15 mL	finely chopped onions
		salt and pepper
		pumpernickel bread
1 tsp	5 mL	black caviar or lumpfish

Combine the eggs, mayonnaise, onion, salt and pepper. Spread on squares of pumpernickel bread and top with the caviar or lumpfish.

A Middle Eastern Love Affair

MENU

LENTIL SOUP

BABA GHANNOUSH
(EGGPLANT PURÉE)

HUMMUS
(CHICK-PEA PURÉE)

PITA BREAD

If winter threatens to banish spring once more, share a Middle Eastern fantasy with your lover. Imagine a camel ride in the desert, a felucca trip down the Nile, a stroll in the valleys of the Holy Land and prepare a mouth-watering Middle Eastern feast.

116

Lentil Soup

1/2 cup	125 mL	dried lentils
	1/2	onion, chopped
	1/2	stalk celery with leaves, chopped
	1/2	medium-sized carrot, chopped
1/2 tsp	2.5 mL	ground cumin
	1	bay leaf, crushed
1/2 tsp	2.5 mL	crushed cardamom seeds
		juice of 1/2 lemon
2 cups	500 mL	beef stock
		salt and pepper to taste
2 tbsp	30 mL	heavy cream

Soak the lentils overnight in cold water. Drain and combine the lentils with the onion, celery, carrot, cumin, bay leaf, cardamom, lemon juice and stock. Bring to a boil, then simmer for 30 minutes. Add salt and pepper. Combine in a blender and purée, adding the cream. Serve hot.

Baba Ghannoush

	1	medium-sized eggplant
		juice of 1 lemon
2 tbsp	30 mL	Sesame Sauce, see below
	1	garlic clove, finely chopped
1 tsp	5 mL	salt
1 tbsp	15 mL	olive oil
1/4 cup	60 mL	finely chopped onion
1 tbsp	15 mL	finely chopped Italian parsley (flat-leaf)
		olive oil, chopped onion and parsley for garnish

Pierce the eggplant in several places with a fork and broil for 20 minutes, turning it to char on all sides. When cooked, peel the eggplant, slice the flesh and combine in a blender with the other ingredients. Chill. Top with olive oil, chopped onion and parsley when ready to serve and accompany with pita bread.

Hummus

1 cup	250 mL	cooked or canned chick-peas, drained and rinsed
1/2 tsp	2.5 mL	salt
	1	garlic clove, finely chopped
		juice of 1/2 lemon
		Sesame Sauce, see below

Combine all the ingredients in a blender and purée. Serve cold on pita bread.

Sesame Sauce

	1	garlic clove, finely chopped
1/2 cup	125 mL	tahina paste (sesame paste, found in gourmet or Middle Eastern shops)
1/2 cup	125 mL	water
		juice of 1/2 lemon
1/2 tsp	2.5 mL	salt

Combine all the ingredients and mix to the consistency of a thick mayonnaise.

There is a private spring to everyone's affection; if you can find that, and touch it, the door will fly open.
THOMAS CHANDLER HALIBURTON

118

Aphrodisiacs in the Spring

MENU

CRAB WRAPPED IN PHYLLO PASTRY
WILD GARLIC CHICKEN
WILD RICE
CHAMPAGNE

What better time for aphrodisiacs than spring! Nature becomes your accomplice, providing you with crustaceans high in love protein and wild garlic, the sorcerer's secret ingredient.

Crab Wrapped in Phyllo Pastry

	1	small can of crab meat, squeezed to drain
1 tbsp	15 mL	sour cream
2 tbsp	30 mL	finely chopped shallots
1 tbsp	15 mL	finely chopped fresh dill (half quantity, if dried)
		juice of 1/4 lemon
		salt and freshly ground pepper
1/4 cup	60 mL	melted butter
	6	sheets of phyllo pastry

Preheat the oven to 350°F (180°C). Combine the crab, sour cream, shallots, dill, lemon juice, salt and pepper in a bowl.

Butter a 2 cup (500 mL) terrine, soufflé or loaf mold. Tear a phyllo sheet into three pieces. Place one piece on the bottom of the mold. Brush with butter. Repeat with more phyllo pieces until you have 9 layers, making sure to butter each layer with a pastry brush. (While assembling the dish, keep the phyllo covered in a damp tea towel to prevent the pastry from drying out.) Spread the crab mixture over the last layer of phyllo. Place and individually butter 9 more layers of phyllo, buttering the last layer as well.

Bake for 30 minutes, or until the pastry puffs up and is golden brown.

Wild Garlic Chicken

3 lb	1.35 kg	chicken
2 tbsp	30 mL	sour cream
1/4 cup	60 mL	finely chopped parsley, thyme, basil and tarragon, combined (half quantity, if dried)
	1	bay leaf, crumbled
		salt and pepper
	20	wild garlic bulbs* (or 10 unpeeled cloves of regular garlic)
2 tbsp	30 mL	olive oil

Preheat the oven to 400°F (205°C). Wash and pat dry the chicken.

---

*Wild garlic is available only in the spring. It is milder than regular garlic and has a slightly different taste.

120

Combine the sour cream, chopped herbs, bay leaf, salt, pepper and half the garlic cloves and place in the cavity of the chicken. Pour the oil into a small roasting pan. Roll the remaining garlic in the oil. Place the chicken on the bed of garlic. Roast for 50 minutes, basting often. Broil for 3 to 4 minutes longer for added crispness and color. Serve with wild rice and a glass of champagne.

Age cannot wither her, nor custom stale
Her infinite variety.
WILLIAM SHAKESPEARE

The Rites of Spring

MENU

CURRIED DEVILLED EGGS
TUNA, TOMATO AND ALFALFA SPROUTS ON RYE
BOURSIN CHEESE WITH UNSALTED CRACKERS
BOCK BEER

Unannounced, the first crocus quietly appears through the windows of the snow and welcomes fearless lovers who brave the cold to greet the sun. The crocus hunt is one of the most enjoyable rites of spring. Share it and this delicious picnic with your lover.

Curried Devilled Eggs

	4	hard-boiled eggs
2 tbsp	30 mL	Homemade Mayonnaise, page 14
	1	green onion, finely chopped
1/2 tsp	2.5 mL	curry powder
		pinch of cayenne pepper
		salt to taste
		fresh parsley for garnish

Cut the eggs in halves lengthwise and remove the yolks. Mash the yolks with a fork and add the mayonnaise, onion, curry, cayenne pepper and salt. Mix thoroughly, then spoon or pipe the mixture into the egg whites. Garnish with parsley. If prepared in advance, keep covered and refrigerated.

Tuna, Tomato and Alfalfa Sprouts on Rye

	1	small can of tuna, drained
2 tbsp	30 mL	Homemade Mayonnaise, page 14
	1/2	celery stalk, finely chopped
	2	spring onions, finely chopped
		juice of 1/2 lemon
		salt and pepper to taste
		rye bread
		alfalfa sprouts
	1	fresh tomato, sliced

Combine the tuna, mayonnaise, celery, onions, lemon juice, salt and pepper. Spread over rye bread. Sprinkle with alfalfa sprouts and top with tomato slices. Accompany with creamy Boursin cheese and bock beer.

Spring hangs her infant blossoms on the trees,
Roc'd in the cradle of the western breeze.
WILLIAM COWPER

Spring Fever Tonic

MENU

VICHYSSOISE
ARTICHOKES STUFFED WITH CRAB
MINERAL WATER OR DRY WHITE WINE

Spring fever has its own particular symptoms and remedies. Even the calmest soul turns restless and romantic with the change of season, but for lovers, spring fever is tantalizing torture. The obvious remedy: a picnic for two.

Vichyssoise

2		large leeks, trimmed of greens and roots
1		onion, chopped
2 tbsp	30 mL	butter
2		medium-sized potatoes, peeled and chopped
2 cups	500 mL	chicken stock
		salt and pepper to taste
1/4 cup	60 mL	heavy cream
1 tsp	5 mL	finely chopped chives or green onion tops

Split the leeks and thoroughly wash between each layer. Chop into bite-sized pieces. In a saucepan over medium heat, sauté the leeks and onions in butter until transparent. Add the potatoes and cook for 5 minutes. Pour in the chicken stock and season with salt and pepper. Bring to a boil, then simmer for 30 minutes.

Transfer the mixture to a blender and blend until smooth. Set aside to cool, then refrigerate. Just before serving, stir in the cream. Serve in chilled bowls, topped with the chopped chives.

Artichokes Stuffed with Crab

2		large globe artichokes
1		lemon
1		bay leaf
1/2 tsp	2.5 mL	sea salt
1		small can of crab meat, drained
2 tbsp	30 mL	sour cream
		juice of 1/2 lemon
1/2 tsp	2.5 mL	finely chopped fresh dill
		pinch of cayenne pepper
		salt to taste

Follow the instructions on page 47 for preparing the artichokes. Cook for 30-40 minutes or until a lower leaf pulls out easily and the meat at the base of the leaf is tender.

Remove the artichokes from the boiling water and drain upside down. Carefully part the leaves of the artichokes and remove the center or hairy choke with a spoon, leaving the outside leaves intact. Combine the crab meat, sour cream, lemon juice and seasonings. Stuff the centers of the warm artichokes with the cold crab mixture and serve immediately. Use the artichoke leaves as spoons to scoop out the crab meat. Don't forget to eat the tender flesh at the base of the leaf as well as the heart at the base of the artichoke. Mineral water could be prescribed for your spring fever, although a glass of well-chilled dry white wine probably would do wonders.

Love conquers all things; let us too surrender to Love.
VIRGIL

Fiddleheads and Firewood

━━◦❖◦⦅❈⦆◦❖◦━━

MENU

GRILLED SPARE-RIBS IN MAPLE SYRUP
POTATOES BAKED IN FOIL
FIDDLEHEADS IN LEMON BUTTER

━━◦❖◦⦅❈⦆◦❖◦━━

Sit by a rushing stream and enjoy the smells and sounds of spring. When you have finished dreaming, take a walk through the woods, pick some fiddleheads and prepare an outdoor barbecue.

Grilled Spare-Ribs in Maple Syrup

1 lb	500 g	spare-ribs
1/4 tsp	1.25 mL	dried sage
1/4 tsp	1.25 mL	dried thyme
		salt and pepper to taste
1/4 cup	60 mL	maple syrup
1/4 tsp	1.25 mL	soya sauce

Rub the spare-ribs with sage, thyme, salt and pepper. Mix together the maple syrup and soya sauce and pour half of the mixture over the spare-ribs. Grill for 30 to 40 minutes over a greased barbecue, basting the ribs with the remaining sauce and turning them often to prevent burning or sticking. Accompany with baked potatoes and fiddleheads in lemon butter.

Fiddleheads in Lemon Butter

1/2 lb	250 g	fresh fiddleheads
2 tbsp	30 mL	butter
		juice of 1/2 lemon
		salt and pepper to taste

Pick fresh fiddleheads on your walk through the woods. (You'll find them near streams in the early spring.) Wash thoroughly and drain. Combine the butter, lemon, salt and pepper. Spread the butter mixture over the fiddleheads. Wrap in foil and steam-cook over the grill for 20 to 30 minutes, or until the fiddleheads are tender-crisp. Serve hot.

The Joys of the First Asparagus

MENU

FRESH ASPARAGUS
SCALLOPS WITH MUSHROOMS AND CREAM
RICE
DRY WHITE WINE

Anticipating the arrival of the first fresh asparagus is one of the great pleasures of spring. But in this case, the reality far surpasses the anticipation. Cooked until just tender and topped with lemony butter, asparagus is almost a meal in itself; combined with scallops and mushrooms, it is a feast.

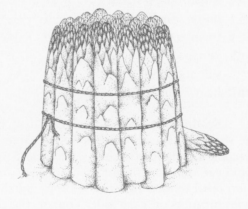

Fresh Asparagus

20		stalks fresh asparagus
3 cups	750 mL	water
3 tbsp	45 mL	butter
2 tbsp	30 mL	bread crumbs
		juice of 1/2 lemon
		salt and pepper to taste

Clean the asparagus, cutting off the tough ends. Tie the asparagus in two bundles and place upright in a pot of boiling salted water. Steam the asparagus until they are just beginning to feel tender. Asparagus should be crisp and not overcooked.

Meanwhile, in a saucepan, melt the butter and thoroughly mix in the bread crumbs, lemon juice, salt and pepper.

Place the cooked asparagus bundles on hot plates, remove the string and pour the hot sauce over the asparagus. Serve immediately.

Scallops with Mushrooms and Cream

2 tbsp	30 mL	butter
1/4 lb	125 g	mushrooms, sliced
1		onion, finely chopped
1/2 lb	250 g	fresh or thawed scallops, cut in halves
1 tbsp	15 mL	chopped fresh parsley
		salt and white pepper to taste
1 tbsp	15 mL	heavy cream

Scallops in cream is an elegant dish, but it is also expensive. To ensure success, have all ingredients prepared and at hand. Take care not to overcook the scallops or they will become tough.

Over medium heat, melt the butter in a saucepan and sauté the mushrooms and onion until tender. Add the scallops, parsley, salt and pepper and cook for two minutes on each side. Pour in the cream and heat for another two minutes. Serve warm with rice, accompanied by a cold dry white wine.

For Continental Lovers

MENU

CONSOMMÉ WITH SHERRY
STEAK AU POIVRE
RICE
ASPARAGUS
PÊCHES AU RHUM

April in Paris. A stroll by the book vendors along the Seine. A picnic in Le Jardin de Luxembourg. Sounds wonderful, even if you are a thousand miles away. Enjoy this picnic on a soft spring night.

Consommé with Sherry

2 cups	500 mL	beef consommé
1 tbsp	15 mL	sherry
1 tbsp	15 mL	freshly chopped parsley and chives, combined
		salt and pepper to taste
		croutons

Thoroughly heat the beef consommé over medium heat. Pour in the sherry and bring to a boil. Reduce to a simmer and add the parsley, chives, salt and pepper. Heat for 5 minutes longer. Serve hot, topped with croutons.

Steak au Poivre

2		small thick steaks, filet or boneless wing
2 tsp	10 mL	crushed peppercorns
1-1/2 tbsp	22.5 mL	butter
1 tbsp	15 mL	flour
1/2 cup	125 mL	beef stock
1 tbsp	15 mL	cognac
2 tbsp	30 mL	heavy cream
		dash of salt
		dash of cognac

Trim and slash the fat of the steaks so that they won't curl as they cook. Pat the crushed peppercorns onto both sides of the steaks. Set the steaks aside while you make the sauce.

Over medium heat, melt the butter, add the flour and stir until brown. Remove from the heat, pour in the stock and stir thoroughly. Return to the heat. Add the cognac, cream and salt and bring to a boil, stirring occasionally. Reduce to simmer and cook for 2 to 3 minutes, until the sauce is creamy. Remove from heat.

Heat a cast-iron skillet. Fry the steaks to desired doneness, gently moving them so that they don't stick to the pan. Do not pierce or press the steaks or you will lose the juices.

When the steaks are nearly done, sprinkle cognac over them and light it with a match. Shake the pan back and forth until the flame goes out. Remove the steaks immediately and keep them warm.

Pour the sauce into the hot skillet and mix with the brown bits. Pour the hot sauce over the steaks and serve at once on warmed plates. Accompany with rice and asparagus.

131

Asparagus

12 stalks of fresh asparagus
    nut of butter
    juice of 1/2 lemon
    salt and pepper to taste

Prepare and cook the asparagus as indicated on page 129. Serve hot topped with butter, lemon juice, salt and pepper.

Pêches au Rhum

		4 fresh or canned peaches
2 tbsp	30 mL	slivered almonds
2 tbsp	30 mL	melted butter
2 tbsp	30 mL	shredded coconut
		juice of 1 lemon
1/4 cup	60 mL	rum
		ice cream

Preheat the oven to 375°F (190°C). Place the peach halves in a baking dish. Combine the almonds, butter and coconut and fill each peach half. Pour the lemon juice and rum over the peaches. Bake for 10 minutes. Serve warm with ice cream.

A Picnic on the Danube

≈◦❀◦❀◦✼◦❀◦❀◦≈

MENU

CANTALOUPE AND PROSCIUTTO
PALACINKY WITH APRICOT OR COTTAGE CHEESE
AND RAISIN FILLING
WHITE DESSERT WINE

≈◦❀◦❀◦✼◦❀◦❀◦≈

The Danube, blue only to lovers, flows peacefully through the historic city of Bratislava. After a Sunday stroll along its green banks, lovers enjoy a sweet Slovak dessert with a glass of white wine. Share this romantic tradition with your lover.

Cantaloupe and Prosciutto

1 ripe cantaloupe
3 slices of prosciutto ham, cut in halves
   juice of 1/2 lemon

Cut the cantaloupe in halves. Remove all the seeds and filaments. Fill the halves with the prosciutto ham and sprinkle with the lemon juice. Serve cold.

Palacinky

1 tbsp	15 mL	melted butter
1 tbsp	15 mL	water
1/2 cup	125 mL	flour
1/2 cup	125 mL	skim milk
1/2 tsp	2.5 mL	salt
1 tbsp	15 mL	sugar
	1	egg
		vegetable shortening
		Cottage Cheese or Apricot Filling, see below

Combine the first 7 ingredients in a blender and purée until smooth. Refrigerate the batter for at least 1 hour.

Heat a skillet or crêpe pan. Melt a dot of vegetable shortening and pour in 2 tbsp (30 mL) of batter. Remove from the heat and tilt the pan in all directions to spread the batter thinly over the surface of the pan. The palacinky should be almost transparent. Return to medium heat and cook for 2 to 3 minutes, or until the bottom of the palacinky is golden brown. Turn and brown the other side. Repeat with the rest of the batter.

Spread some filling over each palacinky, roll and dust with icing sugar.

Apricot Filling

1/2 cup	125 mL	apricot jam
		juice of 1/2 lemon
		icing sugar

Spread the jam over the palacinky. Roll and sprinkle with lemon juice and icing sugar.

Cottage Cheese and Raisin Filling

1/2 cup	125 mL	cottage cheese, drained
1 tsp	5 mL	sugar
	1	egg yolk, lightly beaten
	1	egg white, lightly beaten
1/4 cup	60 mL	raisins
		rind of 1/2 lemon

Combine all ingredients and spread over the palacinky. Roll and sprinkle with icing sugar.

Springtime Fancy

MENU

PANCAKES WITH MAPLE SYRUP
BANANAS AND TANGELOS IN YOGHURT
MINT TEA

''In Spring a young man's fancy turns to thoughts of love''...and breakfast. Indulge your lover with a taste of spring.

Pancakes with Maple Syrup

1/2 cup	125 mL	all-purpose flour
1 tbsp	15 mL	sugar
1 tsp	5 mL	baking powder
	1	egg, beaten
1/2 cup	125 mL	milk
1 tbsp	15 mL	melted butter
		maple syrup

Combine the flour, sugar and baking powder. In a separate bowl, mix the egg, milk and butter. Pour the egg mixture into the dry ingredients and mix well. Butter a skillet and place over medium heat. When the butter is bubbling, pour in one-quarter of the batter and cook until the top of the pancake is filled with bubbles and the bottom is well browned. Turn over to brown the other side. Remove and keep warm. Repeat to make 3 more pancakes. Serve hot topped with maple syrup.

Bananas and Tangelos in Yoghurt

	1	ripe banana, peeled and sliced
	1	tangelo, peeled and sectioned
		juice of 1/2 lemon
1/4 cup	60 mL	natural yoghurt
1 tbsp	15 mL	liquid honey

Sprinkle the banana and tangelo pieces with the lemon juice and combine with the yoghurt. Mix in the honey. Serve cold, with a pot of mint tea.

Spring is come home with her world-wandering feet.
And all things are made young with young desires.
FRANCIS THOMPSON

Love Foods

The love feast is an ancient tradition, immortalized in song and verse and surrounded by legends of love potions for the timid and aphrodisiacs for the amorous. From the beginning of time, lovers have believed in the magical properties of certain foods. Here, for you and your lover, are a few of those legends.

Romantic Herbs and Spices

Certain herbs and spices have enjoyed a privileged place in lore and legend, symbolizing love, passion, jealousy, desire or fidelity. The most romantic myths depict amorous rivalries between the gods or celebrate beauty and love.

The history of the bay or laurel leaf, for instance, involves a tale of pursuit. Apollo, the sun god, fell in love with and pursued a lovely young huntress named Daphne. Fleeing from him, Daphne entreated her father to save her, and mercifully she was changed into a laurel tree. Apollo mourned his loss, and according to Ovid, made the tree his own:

> *Because thou canst be*
> *My mistress, I espouse thee for my tree,*
> *Be thou the prize of honor and renown;*
> *The deathless poet and the poem crown.*
> *Thou shalt the Roman festivals adorn*
> *And, after poets, be by victors worn.*

To this day, the laurel tree is known in Greece as the Daphne Tree.

Jealousy plays a part in the legends surrounding mint. According to myth, Pluto, the god of the underworld, was attracted to the nymph Menthe. In a fit of jealousy, Pluto's wife turned Menthe into the slim green herb we know as mint.

The story of marjoram and oregano (wild marjoram) is a much happier one. Venus, the goddess of love, liked this herb so much that she raised it from the depths of the ocean and grew it on Mount Olympus, close to the sun. She named it Joy of the Mountain.

Basil and rosemary, two herbs immortalized in romantic poetry, are associated with the death of a loved one. Keats in his tragic poem "Isabella or the Pot of Basil" used this association when describing how Isabella hid the severed head of her murdered lover:

> *She wrapp'd it up; and for its tomb did choose*
> *A garden-pot, wherein she laid it by,*
> *And cover'd it with mould, and o'er it set*
> *Sweet Basil, which her tears kept ever wet.*

Rosemary, the traditional symbol of remembrance, appears in Shakespeare's *Hamlet* when grieving Ophelia wails: "There's rosemary, for remembrance, / Pray you, love, remember..." (act 4, scene 5). And cinnamon, too, is associated with loss. As a measure of his grief, Emperor Nero is said to have burned a year's supply of cinnamon at his wife's funeral.

Other herbs and spices were used to "cure" specific love sicknesses. Cumin, for example, reputedly keeps lovers from becoming fickle, while thyme can bring an end to melancholy. Even ordinary pepper has links with romance. It was thought to promote a good disposition in a lover and was also used as a payment in dowries. Saffron, the edible gold, has been steeped in romance since Nefertiti's time.

A Thousand and One Nights

While romantic herbs and spices appealed to the emotions, aphrodisiacs were used to ensure the more sensual pleasures. Early rituals involved brewing love potions while venerating the goddesses of love and fecundity. And references to the effectiveness of aphrodisiacs can be found in the Bible, *The Kama Sutra*, *The Perfumed Garden* of Sheik Nefsaoui, *The Arabian Nights* and *Satyricon*, as well as in Shakespeare and more modern writings.

Magic, mystery, pleasure and satisfaction were, and still are, important components of aphrodisiacs – and so, understandably, is physical well-being. With the exception of a deadly few (the Spanish Fly, for example), many aphrodisiacs are healthy foods which contribute to proper nutritional balance, a point in their favor for today's health-conscious lovers.

For starters, there is rhinoceros horn (good luck in finding one!). It is one of many Chinese aphrodisiacs, along with ginseng in root, tonic or drink form and bird's-nest soup, which is prepared from seaweed and the fish spawn eaten by sea swallows and regurgitated to make their nests. Ginger root, in fresh root or powdered form, is considered an aphrodisiac in both China and India. It is the base for many Indian dishes, as are curry, chutney, mango, ghee (clarified butter) and sesame, all of which are reputed to be effective aphrodisiacs. *The Kama Sutra* recommends that "If ghee, honey, sugar and licorice in equal quantities, the juice of the fennel plant, and milk are mixed together, this nectar-like composition is said to be holy, and provocative of sexual vigour, a preservative of life, and sweet to the taste."

Many herbs and spices are said to ensure amorous vigor. Coriander is mentioned as an aphrodisiac in *A Thousand and One Nights.* Savory, from the Latin *saturya*, was said to have been the chosen plant of satyrs and consequently came to be highly valued. Cloves were used by the Romans, Greeks and Persians as a base in many love philters, and dill and ginger were essential ingredients for most love potions. Other herbs and spices reputed to be effective are celery, parsley, sage, anise, cloves, mustard and lovage (the name itself should do the trick!)

But aphrodisiacs need not be exotic to be effective. Lemons, onions and garlic are popular aphrodisiacs, and all three are used frequently in the recipes in this book. Vegetables such as artichokes, asparagus, mushrooms, truffles, avocado, cucumber, peas, radishes, zucchini and tomatoes (known as love apples) are also frequently cited as love foods. Fruit, on the other hand, is usually considered an accompaniment to a love feast rather than as an aphrodisiac. However, apricots, pomegranates, papaya, grapes, cherries and apples, the earliest symbol of temptation, have all been called the ambrosia of the gods.

Meat rarely figures in aphrodisiac lore, unless it is enhanced by certain herbs and spices as in pepper steak and meat curries. But shellfish such as oysters, mussels, crab, shrimps, scampi and lobster have been considered potent aphrodisiacs throughout the ages. Snails and caviar have a special place in the hearts of lovers.

Not to be forgotten are some of the more traditional aphrodisiacs including wheat germ, pine nuts, almonds, sunflower seeds, raisins, dates, olives, honey, milk and eggs.

Whether you are brewing up a special meal for a seduction or serving a light snack to refresh your lover's passion, don't forget the power of the grape. Choose wines to reflect your mood from this romantic selection: *Les Amoureuses, Les Charmes, Saint-Amour, Puits d'Amour, Cuvée les Amours, Nuits St-Georges,* and *Côtes des Nuits.* Or try a liqueur such as B & B or Advocaat. When all else fails, pour two glasses of champagne, light a fire and enjoy what – with a little luck – will be the first of your 1001 nights.